THE HEART THAT SEES GOD

FRANCIS FRANGIPANE

CHARISMA HOUSE

THE HEART THAT SEES GOD by Francis Frangipane
Published by Charisma House, an imprint of Charisma Media
1150 Greenwood Blvd., Lake Mary, Florida 32746

Copyright © 2024 by Francis Frangipane. All rights reserved.

Unless otherwise noted, all Scripture quotations are taken from
the (NASB®) New American Standard Bible®, Copyright © 1960,
1971, 1977, 1995, 2020 by The Lockman Foundation. Used by
permission. All rights reserved. www.lockman.org

Scripture quotations marked AMP are from the Amplified® Bible
(AMP), Copyright © 2015 by The Lockman Foundation. Used by
permission. www.Lockman.org

Scripture quotations marked AMPC are from the Amplified®
Bible (AMPC), Copyright © 1954, 1958, 1962, 1964, 1965,
1987 by The Lockman Foundation. Used by permission. www.
Lockman.org

Scripture quotations from GOD'S WORD® are copyright ©
1995 God's Word to the Nations. Used by permission of Baker
Publishing Group.

Scripture quotations marked KJV are from the King James
Version of the Bible.

Scripture quotations marked MEV are from the Modern English
Version. Copyright © 2014 by Military Bible Association. Used
by permission. All rights reserved.

Scripture quotations from THE MODERN LANGUAGE BIBLE,
THE NEW BERKLEY VERSION IN MODERN ENGLISH are
Copyright© 1945, 1959, 1969 by Zondervan Publishing House.

Scripture quotations from the NEW ENGLISH BIBLE are
Copyright© 1961, 1970 by Cambridge University Press, Oxford
University Press. All rights reserved.

Scripture quotations marked NIV are taken from the Holy Bible, New International Version®, NIV® Copyright © 1973, 1978, 1984, 2011 by Biblica, Inc.® Used by permission of Zondervan. All rights reserved worldwide. www.zondervan.com. The "NIV" and "New International Version" are trademarks registered in the United States Patent and Trademark Office by Biblica, Inc.®

Scripture quotations marked NKJV are taken from the New King James Version®. Copyright © 1982 by Thomas Nelson. Used by permission. All rights reserved.

While the author has made every effort to provide accurate, up-to-date source information at the time of publication, statistics and other data are constantly updated. Neither the publisher nor the author assumes any responsibility for errors or for changes that occur after publication. Further, the publisher and author do not have any control over and do not assume any responsibility for third-party websites or their content.

For more resources like this, visit charismahouse.com and the author's website at www.frangipane.org.

Cataloging-in-Publication Data is on file with the Library of Congress.
International Standard Book Number: 978-1-63641-102-6
E-book ISBN: 978-1-63641-103-3

1 2024
Printed in the United States of America

Most Charisma Media products are available at special quantity discounts for bulk purchase for sales promotions, premiums, fund-raising, and educational needs. For details, call us at (407) 333-0600 or visit our website at www.charismamedia.com.

THE BEATITUDES

Blessed are the poor in spirit, for theirs
is the kingdom of heaven.
Blessed are those who mourn, for they will be comforted.
Blessed are the meek, for they will inherit the earth.
Blessed are those who hunger and thirst for
righteousness, for they will be filled.
Blessed are the merciful, for they will be shown mercy.
Blessed are the pure in heart, for they will see God.
Blessed are the peacemakers, for they
will be called children of God.
Blessed are those who are persecuted because of
righteousness, for theirs is the kingdom of heaven.
Blessed are you when people insult you, persecute you and
falsely say all kinds of evil against you because of me. Rejoice
and be glad, because great is your reward in heaven, for in the
same way they persecuted the prophets who were before you.

—Matthew 5:3–12, NIV

CONTENTS

PREFACE

I F SOMEONE ASKED ME what the most important teachings of my life are, I would say my sermon series on the Beatitudes, which has been captured in this book. They are always there in the substructure of my hope and walk with God. There is something in these words that I love. To read the Sermon on the Mount is to gaze at the kingdom of heaven. It's to gaze at what heaven is like. It goes the extra mile. It turns the other cheek. It doesn't judge. This is heaven. It's the place we are all preparing to go to; it is in us now, working out its ways, its dynamics, and its life in the context of our human relationships and our relationship with God.

PART I

I CHOSE TO WRITE the majority of part I in narrative, or story, form. My effort here was to capture the atmosphere and excitement of what it could have been like on a personal level for John the Baptist and Jesus coming into their destinies.

CHAPTER 1

THE LAST KINGDOM ON EARTH

*This gospel of the kingdom shall be preached
in the whole world as a testimony to all the
nations, and then the end will come.*

—MATTHEW 24:14

WHEN THE MESSIAH, Jesus Christ, came to our world, so did the kingdom of heaven. Christ did not isolate His message to one or two aspects of the kingdom. The headline "Repent, for the kingdom of heaven is at hand" (Matt. 4:17) was an invitation to purify our hearts that we might see the face of God and experience the wondrous glory of heaven on earth.

In the kingdom, there was salvation, healing, forgiveness, power, destiny, hope, and revival. *The kingdom of God was the ship that carried the cargo of divine blessings into the world of men.*

Jesus said before His second coming there would also be a second manifestation of heaven (Dan. 2:44). Just as the power and life of heaven accompanied the Lord in earthly ministry, this same heavenly life would similarly empower and flow through His people in the last years of this age.

Signs and wonders, as heralds of His imminent return, would accompany the proclaiming of His message. He said, "This gospel of the kingdom shall be preached in the whole world as a testimony to all the nations, and then the end will come" (Matt. 24:14).

We are not to confuse the gospel of salvation with the gospel of the kingdom.

Salvation is a foundational dimension of spiritual life; it is part of the kingdom gospel. Salvation is a gift: believe and be saved. *The kingdom gospel, however, costs us.* We cannot serve two masters; the kingdom gospel is a treasure hidden in a field. It costs us our all but gives us God's best. It includes not only all the verses modern Christians highlight in their Bibles but also those we skim or ignore because they are *unattainable* until our focus lifts to the standards of God's kingdom.

One might argue that most of the world has heard the gospel. Yes, they have heard about Jesus; they have also heard about salvation and forgiveness, but few have seen the demonstrated power of the gospel of the kingdom. Yet that is precisely what Jesus said would be revealed before His return. He said, *"this* gospel," meaning *His* gospel as He taught and demonstrated it. Is it possible that the kingdom of heaven is near enough to reach from where we are?

THE GOD OF HEAVEN

To those who love Christ and follow Him, the reality of heaven will become increasingly visible. Not only will there be more miracles, but there will be wonders in the heavens and signs on earth (Acts 2:19). Interestingly, this revelation concerning the establishment of God's kingdom at the end of the age was also revealed to King Nebuchadnezzar through the prophet Daniel. God gave Nebuchadnezzar a dream in which he saw the sequence of kingdoms that would rule the earth, beginning with his own. What is pertinent to us is the last kingdom.

Read what Daniel the prophet said would occur during the era of the last kings on earth:

> The God of heaven will set up a kingdom that will never be destroyed, and that kingdom will not be left for another people; it will crush and end all these kingdoms, but it will endure forever.
>
> —DANIEL 2:44

Consequently, when Jesus told His disciples that the gospel of the kingdom would be proclaimed worldwide, He referred to this prophecy in Daniel. The full establishment of this kingdom will not occur until after Jesus returns, but we feel its beginnings now.

As we stand before the Lord in our day, we are aware of the darkness covering the earth, and deep darkness its people, but let us stay focused, for certainly among all the signs of the end—increasing wickedness, geophysical trauma (earthquakes), lawlessness, and despair—the God of heaven is simultaneously setting up His kingdom. For behold, the kingdom of heaven is at hand.

CHAPTER 2

HEAVEN WITHIN OUR REACH

Repent, for the kingdom of heaven is at hand.
—MATTHEW 4:17

THE AUTUMN SUN shimmered off the Jordan's waters, but no light shone brighter than the blaze within the prophet's spirit. John's fire was fueled by the inextinguishable call of apocalyptic significance from birth. Even before Jesus was born, the archangel Gabriel heralded his birth and subsequent ministry (Luke 1:11–20). John's conception came supernaturally to parents "advanced in years" (v. 7).

John's priestly father, Zacharias, experienced miracles of judgment and supernatural deliverance, all of which sounded a trumpet of anticipation concerning John's unique call from God.

Israel's priesthood guarded and trained the prophet as a small child. In obedience to the angelic decree, John was set apart to the Almighty as a Nazarite from birth: no razor would ever touch his hair, nor alcohol wet his lips.

As an adolescent, John's quest to grasp and identify his destiny compelled him from his home in Judah's hill country to ever-extended seasons of isolation and desolation in the Judean wilderness. He would eventually spend nearly two-thirds of his life in the wilderness with the Word of God and the howling silence of the desert as his constant companions.

To John, the sacred scrolls were more than the depository of divine truth; they also detailed his extraordinary mission. If, as the angel said in verse 17, he would "go as a forerunner" before the Lord, surely he would find scriptures that would route him toward his destiny. Was he Elijah? Was he the prophet spoken of by Moses? Or was he the messenger of the covenant referred to by the prophet Malachi? The answer to this question, he felt, would be the key to unlocking the Messiah's return.

Indeed, when his ministry began, the multitudes asked, "Are you Elijah?"

He replied, "I am not."

"Are you the Prophet?" they queried, speaking of the One who would lead Israel in the stature of Moses.

He again answered, "No."

"Who are you?" they entreated. "What do you say about yourself?" (vv. 21–22).

Years in the blazing wilderness had refined John of all things nonessential. Distilled by the Spirit to his truest essence, he discovered his role in the book of the prophet Isaiah.

Then the word of the Lord came to John in the desert. He was "the voice of one crying in the wilderness: 'Prepare the way of the Lord; make His paths straight'" (Luke 3:4, MEV). He would prepare the way for the coming of the Messiah.

Months had passed, and the Baptizer and his disciples had traversed the upper and lower Jordan valley, stopping for a time at Aenon near Salim, where the river spread out and deepened. Here, he could baptize the ever-increasing numbers who followed him.

Indeed, everywhere the Baptizer went, he compelled the multitudes with the same powerful message:

"Repent, for the kingdom of heaven is at hand" (Matt. 3:2). Heaven? At hand? If something was at hand, it was close enough to reach, near enough to touch and enter from where men dwelt.

But could heaven truly be accessible? Perhaps to prophets who dwelt in deserts, but to common men and women? Israel's tradition was a religion about God. For centuries, the Jewish priests served God's presence, first in a small inner room in a portable tabernacle and then more permanently in their temple, but the prophet proclaimed that heaven itself was nearby.

For more than a thousand years, the prophets preceding John had predicted a great era of spiritual confrontation and fulfillment, a time when the nations would experience the inheritance of the Lord. Yes, numerous psalms also heralded the glorious time when the nations would bow in worship before Yahweh, God of Israel. Indeed, was not Abraham called the "father of many nations" (Rom. 4:17)? Isaiah wrote of a time when the nations would come to God's light. Daniel, Ezekiel, Jeremiah, and the minor prophets announced the "great and terrible day of the LORD" (Joel 2:31, AMP). It was a period when the entire earth would be subdued and reunited under God's sovereignty.

John was convinced that Jesus' baptism would precipitate this long-awaited kingdom. The Lord had not assigned John the task of establishing the kingdom, only preparing the way. He was the herald, not the builder. God did not reveal to the prophet the details of how the kingdom would come. The Spirit had not told John what to look for but whom.

CHAPTER 3

THE REDEMPTION HYMN BEGINS

*Behold, My Servant, whom I uphold; My chosen one
in whom My soul delights. I have put My Spirit upon
Him; He will bring forth justice to the nations.*

—Isaiah 42:1

ABOUT SIX MONTHS after the Baptizer proclaimed the kingdom of God was at hand, a carpenter in a small Judean village put away His tools and swept His woodworking shop for the last time. Shrouded in the obscurity of a commoner's occupation, the Messiah of Israel knew, at long last, the fullness of His time had come.

He possessed no stately form, no outer majesty to which people would be drawn. Beneath the plain exterior of this humble carpenter was a heart of inestimable worth; to heaven, here was the incomparable pearl of great price. Perfectly vulnerable to the voice and power of love, the carpenter recognized the potential for redemption in everything. Just as He took dead, dried wood and transformed it into a thing of beauty and purpose, He recognized the potential of transformation even in the most barren of souls. He was full of joy, uniquely childlike in spirit, and profoundly ancient in wisdom.

Completely uncluttered by insecurity, ambition, or jealousy, the woodworker fulfilled the heart of God. It was time for the One who would be known to the Gentile world as Jesus to begin His ministry and receive His heavenly inheritance.

Jesus routinely prayed in the hills west of Nazareth. That evening He returned to the hills and the embrace of His heavenly Father's love.

The next morning the Nazarene rose before dawn, dressed, and left for the Jordan River. Thirty years of preparation—learning obedience to God's voice, suffering the deep lessons of love, and, perhaps most significant, wrestling with the burden of an unfathomable destiny—all settled into Jesus' stride as He walked the dry, narrow path toward the Jordan. The magnitude of the Father's pleasure enveloped the carpenter like a spectacular garment of light.

From the time John's ministry exploded onto the nation, there had been an ever-increasing stir of spiritual activity in the Messiah's life. John's message of repentance was to precede Jesus' arrival, and that miraculous power would shortly accompany His life.

Yet during this time, Jesus was also reacquainted with grief. Sorrows, such as those that grip a heart made defenseless by love, had accompanied the Nazarene. These recent months were no exception, for His time had not yet come.

As the time for His public ministry approached, a deep rest began to descend on the Galilean. His life energies, visions, and virtues came together, tuned like the instruments of symphony musicians before their grand performance—each virtue calibrated to perfect pitch, each righteous passion lifted to its highest power. To the casual eye, Jesus' external life might have seemed like a canopy of discordant experiences. In truth, the powerful graces that worked so deeply throughout this time—the perseverance and peace, the fear of God and fearless love of people, both

His humility and authority—were summoned to perfect synchrony and heightened fullness.

As this day dawned, Jesus was fully aware that the great conductor of His life, the heavenly Father, had risen. His baton was in His hand. As He tapped the podium's edge, all the holy aspects of Jesus' soul were worshipfully subdued, reduced to focused silence and surrender. Within the hallowed concert hall of this most sacred life, surrounding angels watched and held their breath. The arms of God Almighty slowly rose and lifted high. The wait was over. The eternal symphony, Christ's redemption hymn, would begin.

CHAPTER 4
THE FORERUNNER

Among those born of women there has not
risen anyone greater than John.
—MATTHEW 11:11, NIV

THE RECENT ARRIVALS packed themselves
along the uppermost of the Jordan River's
descending banks; a human tributary flowed
out from the group and along the twisting path to
the river's edge. Since early dawn, the gathering had
steadily increased. Now late morning, hundreds of
people were pressed together beneath the hot Judean
sun. Overhead, a falcon circled, cocked its head, and
repeatedly screeched at the encroaching crowd.

Along the dry, twisting path to the Jordan, still
more of the unbaptized came: some in clusters, others
as pairs, and some alone. The path opened to a flat
clearing that widened toward a slightly terraced
embankment. Each person had come for one irre-
pressible reason: to hear the prophet of God.

Eventually, nearly every adult from Jerusalem, Judea,
and throughout the district of the Jordan would trek
into this forbidding wilderness. Compelled by holy
fear, they came. Urged along by the pressing grip of
destiny, they hastened toward the prophet's voice,
and the lone distinguishable sound of the falcon that
soared above the multitudes.

Israel was the land of prophets. By a prophet the
Lord brought Israel out of Egypt, and by a prophet He
preserved the nation. In contrast, philosophers and
generals escorted the Greeks into history; astrologers
and kings guided the Persians. The Hebrews' destiny
was irreversibly fused to Yahweh, their God, and His
servants, the prophets. Indeed, from generation to

generation, in message after message, the prophetic voice hammered the will of God into the cultural matrix of Israel's identity.

The prophets were living symbols of Yahweh's love. They burned with the fire of divine jealousy. Sometimes harsh, always unswerving, fought and resisted as they were, the prophets were a gift from God to the Hebrews. Nearly four hundred years had passed with little to no words from the prophets. Now, the "voice of God" returned, and ancient longings were awakened within a chosen people.

The one known as the Baptizer stood waist-deep in the muddy river. His thirty years of uncut hair, wet with sweat and brown river water, clung like a mantle over the middle of his back and shoulders; his equally long beard flowed almost seamlessly into the rust-brown fur of his camel-skin garment. Standing with him in the water, in a row parallel with the embankment, were his disciples, each listening to, praying with, and then baptizing the repentant Jews.

These were days of great fear and greater expectation; the awe of prophetic fulfillment and anticipation struck both men and women. Indeed, the multitudes knew God had sent John as His prophet and empowered his message. The Baptizer accommodated no hidden fear of offending the weakened sensibilities of his generation. He led no one in a quiet every-head-bowed, every-eye-closed prayer. He insisted on an open, audible confession of sin as a manifestation of heartfelt abhorrence of evil. Diplomacy and discretion were fugitives in the fiery world of the prophetic word; tact, to John, was merely cultured deceit. He used none of it.

Standing along the Jordan's uppermost ridge were the Pharisees, Israel's religious elite. They had not come to humble themselves but to observe and criticize. The Pharisees were a caste of eminent religious leaders. Among them were the scribes—copyists, editors, and learned teachers of Israel's Law—several of whom also served as priests in the temple ritual. The Pharisees believed in the resurrection, angels, and miracles; they diligently kept the Sabbath and faithfully tithed even their garden herbs. On their foreheads and wrists, secured by leather straps, were small boxes called phylacteries, which contained key scriptures from the Law.

The Pharisees rose as a sect nearly two hundred years before John's arrival. They emerged as successors to the Maccabees, a family of warring priests who defended the Jewish culture from the Syrian attempt to unite the known world under the domination of Hellenism. The name Pharisees means "the separate ones"[1] and embodied their quest to keep Israel from Gentile contamination. Yet in time, the Pharisees positioned themselves as detached and above even their countrymen.

As John and his disciples baptized people in the ravine below, the Pharisees arrived but remained aloof. Each stood with his arms folded as various scribes jotted questions and challenges about John's doctrine. The Pharisees had seated themselves in the chair of Moses; considering themselves the guardians of Israel's religious traditions, they disdained this new rite of baptism.

"We've had washings and cleansings, but this crude baptism of John's is without precedent!" they argued. "The sacred scrolls are closed books. We need no new understanding of truth," they charged.

Their self-righteousness immunized them from the fever of John's passions. The prophet detested the religious and cultural arrogance of these leaders. Sheltered comfortably within the stronghold of their religious pride, their souls were watertight against the waves of humility and godly sorrow—and expectation—sweeping the nation.

John had been preaching to the multitude, but now he turned his gaze toward the Pharisees. He pointed at them, his eyes seeing through the outer pretension of their religiosity, penetrating each heart's dark, twisted attitudes. "Brood of vipers!" he thundered. "Who warned you to flee from the wrath to come?" (Luke 3:7, NKJV). They thought of themselves as mountains and hills among men, yet Yahweh promised all who exalt themselves shall be brought low (Luke 14:11).

The Pharisees, who, except for a few who felt conviction, were the primary target of John's words, saw and felt nothing except an ever-hardened coldness around their hearts.

John's proclamation against the "mountains" of pride and self-righteousness did not end his assault against sin. Indeed, there were also valleys within human nature: dark, subterranean regions of oppression and spiritual paralysis created through fear, moral failure, and self-pity.

The prophet's gaze now turned toward these low places within the hearts of the multitude. Flashing like lightning, his eyes subdued the internal sentinels of compromise and guilt that held hostage the will of many. A holy expectation rose, trembling as it came—its name was hope. The living God had returned to Israel.

This was not ritual or religion but complete submission to the reign of Yahweh. Indeed, no baptized person pretended repentance that they did not passionately and desperately encounter. Many of the freshly baptized remained downstream, unable to remove themselves from the baptismal area. They stood with hands trembling, engulfed in holy sorrow. The living God had exposed the wretchedness of sin on their souls and was now, in tenderness, removing it.

Daily the Baptizer spoke, and daily the multitudes left their homes and villages to walk into the forbidding wilderness. They came knowing they would weep and wail and grieve for their iniquities.

Still, they were drawn toward more than just attaining contrition. Repentance was but half of the prophet's message. Their hearts were fraught and pounding with the anticipation of John's earnest proclamation: the kingdom of heaven was at hand!

CHAPTER 5

GOD ON EARTH

You are My beloved Son; in You I am well-pleased.

—MARK 1:11

THE JORDAN RIVER was miles from Nazareth, and yet Jesus walked even farther beyond the Jordan to Bethany, where John was baptizing. In the late afternoon, Jesus took His place at the rear of the crowd. Following the movement of the gathering, the Nazarene stepped forward and down the embankment until He reached the small clearing by the river's edge. Pausing, He stepped into the current, His eyes on the Baptizer.

John's mind flashed back to that momentous day when the word of the Lord came to him in the wilderness in a blaze of living glory. There, in the wastelands of the desert, the Spirit of the almighty God enveloped the prophet as John became a man "sent from God" (John 1:6). Now, the same awe gripped his heart; the living glory was descending again. The air itself was charged with divine life, pulsing with waves of eternal light so bright and consuming that everything disappeared except the man before him.

John's gaze tunneled into Jesus' heart. John's penetrating vision saw that, unlike all who had come previously, this heart had no sin. His eyes raced to the corners of Jesus' soul. There was no arrogance, no lust, no fear, no pride. Of the ten thousand people the prophet's spirit scanned, never had he beheld such utter purity of heart.

Yet, even beyond the carpenter's innocence, John was staggered by something more wonderful than he had ever known. Here was one not only conformed to God's laws but conformed to His love.

John's message had always been as fierce as the hot desert sun and as harsh as his camel-hair garment. His words were a hammer that shattered the hardness of men's hearts. John caused men to fear; Jesus caused men to hope. Standing before the prophet was the perfection of love—masculine, confident, and utterly disarming.

As fearless as John was, he had long since resolved to speak truth at the peril of his life. Persecution, suffering, hardship, and rejection—John reveled in them as signs of his authenticity.

To suffer for God was a prophetic privilege. Yet John knew that in Jesus' presence even the worst sinner could find shelter. Not only did the sanctity of Jesus stun the prophet, but the sanctuary of Jesus' countenance also overwhelmed him. John could be honest with his own need and not find rejection or condemnation waiting.

Jesus lifted His eyes from the water and looked at John. Forgetting the waning crowds and ignoring his attending disciples, John could not restrain himself.

"I have the need to be baptized by You," he cried (Matt. 3:14).

Jesus placed His hand gently on the prophet's chest and calmed the trembling in John's soul. In a voice that was almost a whisper, the Anointed One of Israel entreated the Baptizer, "It is vital that you baptize Me;

for in this way we will both fulfill all righteousness."
(See Matthew 3:15.)

At that, Jesus knelt before John in the water.
Reluctantly, John put his hands on the carpenter's
shoulders and, leaning backward, immersed Him in
the river. As He rose from the water, the heavens above
Him opened, and the Holy Spirit descended and gently
rested on the Messiah's shoulders.

John had once sought the Almighty concerning the
details of the Messiah's appearance: What would the
Anointed of God look like? Would He come from the
priesthood, or would He be a prophet whose spiritual experience was like John's, whom the Almighty
also trained in the desert? Would He arrive violent in
nature, girded with a sword as captain of the Lord's
host? Many false messiahs had already surfaced in
Israel. Thus, in earnest he sought to know how he
would recognize the true Messiah.

The Almighty had given John a confirming sign:
"He upon whom you see the Spirit descending and
remaining upon Him, this is the One who baptizes in
the Holy Spirit" (John 1:33).

Now, at the Jordan the sign was fulfilled. The Father
spoke audibly concerning Jesus, and John heard the
voice of God. "This is My beloved Son, with whom I
am well pleased."

In a mystery that transcends human understanding,
for the only time in history, the nature of God was

revealed on earth as He is in heaven: Father, Son, and Holy Spirit.

As a result of his encounter with Jesus, the deep restlessness within the prophet had ceased. The change was unnoticed by the multitudes but recognized by his disciples. Ever so slightly, the intensity of John's spirit relaxed, not as though he had withdrawn but rather arrived at a transfer point in the unfolding of God's kingdom. Indeed, from this point onward, John knew that his influence must decrease while the Messiah's would increase. It was well with John's soul, for the Anointed of Israel had arrived at last.

John's power blazed through his words, his gaze, and his spirit. He was sent to prepare the way through a baptism of repentance, and this he did. But the power accompanying the Messiah would be greater yet; He came to immerse Israel in the life substance of God Himself! Such authority was unfathomable to the prophet. The thought staggered him. Now that he had seen the heart of Christ—so spiritually pure, so full of compassion, so altogether different and outside expectations—John's awe of God expanded. He knew that in seeing the Lord's Messiah, he was gazing upon the face of God Himself.

CHAPTER 6

PERFECT SURRENDER

*Jesus came into Galilee, preaching the gospel of God,
and saying, "The time is fulfilled, and the kingdom
of God is at hand; repent and believe in the gospel."*

—MARK 1:14–15

JESUS STILL LOOKED like a carpenter. He wore the same clothes. His hair and beard had not changed. His hands were still calloused. He still walked with the same steady gait. Yet inwardly, the resplendent glory of the Father had expanded to full zenith. His years of training, learning obedience through suffering, and maintaining perfect purity in all things bloomed in unblemished oneness with God. The Almighty had not merely given Jesus a plan; He gave the richest access to Himself.

The heart of Christ was so perfectly surrendered that He could gaze on the Father with unfiltered clarity. In this secret place of the Most High, this abode between life temporal and life eternal, Jesus beheld the activity of God. What He saw and heard in secret from His Father, He repeated publicly before men. As such, Israel's Messiah lived in perfect synchrony with the Father's passions. Just as the Israelites had followed the pillar of God's glory in the wilderness, Jesus fully aligned His life so that in all things His sole pursuit was His Father's glory.

When the Most High called His Son to spend His nights in prayer, Jesus did so. When He required of Him forty days without food in the wilderness, Jesus complied. When starvation or obedience to God was His choice, Jesus stayed true to the Father's will even when weak and tempted by Satan.

Only after a night on a mountain with God did Jesus select as "special messengers" those twelve whom the Father named. He obeyed, knowing their frailties, fears, and ambitions, fully aware that a thief among them would later betray Him.

When the need for miracles of healing or deliverance arose, Jesus never acted in presumption or self-will, no matter how desperate the situation was. If, in prayer, Jesus recognized the Father's readiness to heal, no matter the size of the multitude, He repeated the healing procedure God gave Him and healed them all. Or, if the Father's choice was to bypass the multitude to heal just one, no matter how hurting the others were, Jesus reached to heal only the one.

Except to position Himself in perpetual oneness with the Father, Jesus did nothing on His own initiative. *All He accomplished and everything He taught was the consequence of His unbroken intimacy with God.* Jesus' goal was not to be "good" in and of Himself but yielded. He had long since identified self-will and independence as enemies to His abiding in the Father's pleasure. His disciples would often substitute self-reliant ideas and actions for true faith. In time, by Christ's example and power, they also learned the futility of trying to serve God without first hearing from God.

Jesus, however, would not test the Father with presumptuous acts. He knew the difference between faith, which came as a response to the Father's voice, and self-willed religion, which could imitate faith but was impotent to effect lasting change.

At the root of Jesus' power was not the hope to work miracles or even the desire to relieve human suffering;

His first goal in everything was to please God. Whatever the Father asked, Jesus did, choosing to define success in terms of God's praise rather than man's.

As a result, the Father gave His Spirit to Christ without measure, and miracles increased in power and number. Each miracle brought Jesus greater fame. Soon, throngs of Jews from Jerusalem, Judea, and beyond the Jordan were flocking to the Messiah to be taught, healed, and delivered. As the miracles increased, news of His power spread to the Gentiles also. Multitudes came from Galilee and Samaria, Decapolis, and then all of Syria, bringing to Him the diseased and pain-ridden, the demoniacs, epileptics, and paralytics. Jew and Gentile alike came to Jesus, and He restored myriads to vibrant health.

After Jesus' baptism by John and subsequent testing in the wilderness, He left His home base in Nazareth and relocated to Capernaum. Awaking early, He walked to the Sea of Galilee. He loved the sound of the gulls, the gentle, rhythmic wash of the small waves, and the smell of the sea air. Hundreds of boats and an equal number of fishermen sorting their catch or trimming nets after a night of fishing dotted the Galilean shoreline.

Fishermen were rowdy, boastful, competitive, honest, and approachable. Perhaps that's why the first four disciples were fishermen. Several who knew Him paused from their work and joined Him on the shore, talking and laughing. As the sun grew hotter, He bid them farewell and walked toward the hills west of

Capernaum. A significant number of fishermen and others from the surrounding villages followed. His disciples also arrived, and by midday quite a gathering had assembled.

Yet His intent was not to minister but to train His disciples. Seeing the ever-increasing multitudes, Jesus ascended a nearby mountain. His steps were as significant now as they were walking to John's baptism.

It was one thing to reveal the miraculous acts of God, demonstrating healing and deliverance to the multitudes; it was another thing to reveal the *ways* of God by training His select disciples.

PART II

I N PART II, THE TRAINING TRANSITIONS to direct teachings on the stages and sequences of the Beatitudes.

CHAPTER 7

THE DISCIPLES

When Jesus saw the crowds, He went up on the mountain; and after He sat down, His disciples came to Him. And He opened His mouth and began to teach them.

—MATTHEW 5:1–2

A TRUE DISCIPLE WILL soon discover there are no shortcuts to the process of Christlikeness; there are only ways to prolong it.

Now seeing the multitudes, the Master ascended a nearby mountain, and as He sat, His disciples came to Him (Matt. 5:1).

While this initial session with the Lord may have included the curious from among the multitudes, the Lord's primary goal was to train His disciples. His theme was direct: He came to plant a colony of heaven among the cultures of men.

The Messiah was Jewish by birth but eternal by nature. Yes, Christ spoke of the Mosaic Law, but His goal was to probe deeper into the hidden layers of the heart. What He came to establish was not a cultural subset of Judaism; He came to plant heaven on earth. Thus, not only would His followers need to know His doctrine, but they would also need to know the life of heaven and display both His power and His character.

But how would the Lord bring His disciples into true spiritual life? They were unlike Him in nearly every way. He was sinless; they were sinful. He was powerful; they were weak. He was surrendered while they were ambitious. Their transformation, by necessity, would be a process.

Yet as Jesus began to train His followers, He made it clear that there would be spiritual milestones along the way, markers by which the disciples could measure themselves.

Matthew 5:2 says, "He opened His mouth and began to teach them." As He did, the most powerful words ever uttered began to accomplish their magnificent objective: conforming humanity's heart to the standards of Christ. Indeed, in what we today call the Beatitudes, we find the secret to inner transformation.

A true disciple will soon discover there are no shortcuts to the process of Christlikeness; there are only ways to prolong it.

STAGES

If the title of Christ's ministry was "Repent, for the kingdom of heaven is at hand," and if the body of His instruction truly focused on the ways of the kingdom, the Beatitudes represented the unfolding stages of kingdom life.

Consider the first beatitude concerning the poor in spirit; Jesus says, "theirs is the kingdom of heaven" (Matt. 5:3). He does not say, "They will go to heaven." He says, "Theirs *is* the kingdom" (present tense). At the close of the Beatitudes, again, Jesus tells those persecuted and slandered for righteousness's sake that "theirs *is* the kingdom of heaven. Again, present tense.

Our journey begins with the assurance of entering heaven after death. (See John chapter 3.) Christ proclaimed this realm called heaven has come to us on planet Earth. The way in is through the person of Christ, who is manifest to us through the Holy Spirit. Through Jesus Christ, heaven is no longer distant; it is "at hand"—close enough to reach from where we stand.

Our Lord began His instruction with what we have come to call the Beatitudes. The word simply means attitudes we are to be. Our first phase will follow Jesus' teaching, incorporating the initial four beatitudes into a season of repentance. Our goal is to be broken, humble, and hungry for God's Word.

> *Lord, I'm a disciple of Jesus Christ. I'm in the process of change, and I ask You to continue giving me the grace to change as I read these words and allow them to do their work in my heart. Help me see the truth about myself so I can experience Your kingdom on earth as it is in heaven. Amen.*

CHAPTER 8
THE BEATITUDES

And He opened His mouth and began to teach them.
—MATTHEW 5:2

ccording to the Gospel of Matthew, the first thing Jesus taught was, "Repent, for the kingdom of heaven is at hand" (Matt. 4:17). The next thing He taught was the Beatitudes. This connection is not coincidental; the Beatitudes represent the attitudes of those who possess the kingdom of heaven. They are not commands; they represent the spiritual dimensions that one should expect to experience as heaven unfolds in their life.

Each beatitude represents a spiritual attainment and is identified by a particular grace and unique blessedness. They are not attainments reached from human initiative or perspective. Rather, they represent divine accomplishments. These are the inner works of God, established by the Holy Spirit in the heart of the Christ follower. And yes, the believer must apply himself and cooperate with the working of grace, but this is the work of God, not man. *The believer should know that the goal of heaven is not only to provide for us but also to perfect us.*

To be blessed is to be shaped inwardly by God. Just as His hands shaped Adam, He reworks the soul of each of His followers, redesigning our thoughts and imaginations and reconfiguring our attitudes until the day we are transformed into His image. We see that to be blessed is not merely to enjoy an increase in financial or material goods; it is to become a living habitation for the Most High.

Indeed, within the heart that God designs, God abides.

INTERCONNECTED, LIVING REALITIES

The Beatitudes represent interconnected realities, divinely sequenced so that the truth of one becomes the substructure for the truth that follows. In other words, the merciful would not know the fullness of God's mercy had they not understood true meekness, which is the result of seeing their poverty of spirit and subsequent mourning for their sin. Nor would there ever be genuine purity of heart without first becoming merciful and hungering and thirsting for righteousness.

Of course, the truth presented in each verse of the Beatitudes stands on its own merit. Many Christians have matured spiritually without ever seeing the divine sequence I write about. Seeing the Beatitudes expressed as a whole rather than unrelated individual pieces reveals a profound benefit to us. Indeed, when these coalesce—as they become the Beatitudes—they create a symphony of divine truth. Not only are they listed together; they fit together.

When Paul writes that "God causes all things to work together for good" (Rom. 8:28), we think his address refers to the effect of God's wisdom and power on a believer's life, and such it is. Yet we also see another parallel truth in this verse, less sublime or quoted than the first but just as true: the creative action of God causes all things to work together. Whenever God is seen, either in creation or in human life, all things work together. Within the Godhead the three work together; within the church the body works together; and here in the Beatitudes we see the working together, the connectedness and harmony of the Beatitudes.

Consider the reward of living in the first beatitude: "Theirs is the kingdom of heaven." He does not promise something limited to eternity; He says, "Theirs *is* the kingdom." It is both now and in eternity. The last beatitude concludes with the same promise.

A present manifestation of heaven on earth comes as God's life unfolds in the lives of His disciples. Each beatitude creates a spiritual reality that, once accepted and established, becomes the entrance into the following beatitude.

How does God purpose to transform us? He begins our inner change by focusing us on our attitudes. If we change our attitudes, we change our perception; our actions and, ultimately, our future all transform according to the attitudes of our hearts. Yet Christ isn't seeking merely to give us different attitudes; He seeks to work in us heaven's attitudes.

Today is similar to the era when Christ first came. Jesus sees the vast numbers of people about to come to Him, and in preparation He is drawing His disciples unto Himself to train them. Remember, Christ's goal is not simply to teach us His doctrine; in everything Jesus Christ presents to us, He ultimately seeks to transfer the fullness of His anointing and power.

Therefore, His disciples were called to literally represent heaven, which is embodied in the person of Christ. They weren't called to start twelve independent denominations. Jesus didn't say, "Christianity is at hand," or, "Judaism is at hand." No. He said, "Repent, for the kingdom of heaven is at hand."

If we intend to do the will of God on earth, we must have a revelation of what God is doing: *Christ came to establish heaven on earth.*

We may not know what the resplendent life of God is like in heaven—what it means to abide in a realm where there is no death, sorrow, or sickness. However, we do know the attitudes of those in heaven. And it is these attitudes that allow the life of heaven to extend to the followers of Christ on earth.

> *Lord, as I study each beatitude and grow into new stages of spiritual maturity, I ask You to transform my soul and plant the attitude of those in heaven deep within me.*

CHAPTER 9

THE POOR IN SPIRIT

*Blessed are the poor in spirit, for theirs
is the kingdom of heaven.*
—Matthew 5:3, NIV

JESUS DOES NOT postpone heaven until after we die; He extends heaven into the world where we live. The "kingdom of heaven" *belongs* to the poor in spirit. God's kingdom has two manifestations: what is partially revealed now in our hearts' attitudes and what is consummate in the eternal life to come. Jesus says that access to heaven is present for the poor in spirit.

If this is so, it behooves us to know what sort of poorness or "poverty" leads to heaven. Certainly, a blessing rests on those who, though poor, are "rich in faith" (Jas. 2:5). Yet poverty itself is not a blessing. No. The Holy Spirit has a larger, more relevant answer to our question about the poor in spirit.

Remember, Jesus is talking to His disciples. He sees multitudes and nations eventually coming into the kingdom, but His quest is to prepare His disciples to represent Him. Thus, His conversation on the mountain is not with vast multitudes but with the small crowd of His disciples.

When Jesus speaks of the "poor in spirit," it refers to a certain spiritual condition He seeks to establish in His disciples' hearts. He is saying, "Blessed are they who know their spiritual need."

The beginning, or entrance, into the realm of heaven comes with the self-discovery of our need for God. In truth everyone in heaven knows their need. In the world without God, self-discovery is often devastating. Yet with the Almighty it is the beginning of all transformation. It is the first blessing the Son of God pronounces to His followers.

We must read the Beatitudes not just with our intellect but with revelation, as though we were there sitting at His feet. Jesus is providing the stages of spiritual growth, and the first gate into the life of heaven is knowing our need.

The Word is living, active, sharper than a sword, piercing and judging even the thoughts and intentions of our hearts. Yes, the Word comforts and encourages us, but if we are even slightly honest, the Word has made us aware that we are often motivated by vain and selfish impulses. We instinctively act more out of fear than faith. Do we believe our hearts' intentions are always pure and Jesus does not need to confront us? Have you truly never been pierced in the heart by the sword of the Word?

Jesus could have warned that unless our righteousness exceeds that of the scribes and Pharisees, we wouldn't be able to enter the kingdom of heaven. Yet of Himself, He said, "Why do you call Me good? No one is good except God alone" (Mark 10:18).

How could Jesus say none were good? Christ models the way of righteousness; He is the face of all goodness on earth. Yet even Christ's goodness is appropriated from God. It is a righteousness that gains access to our hearts through partnership with the Almighty.

The beginning of all transformation is knowing

what needs to change within us. We cannot be set free from anything we cannot see and identify as sin.

The past cannot be forgotten; it can only be redeemed. We sin and think that in time the penalty of sin will fade. However, sin has burrowed into us, establishing itself as a living part of our soul.

And more, each beatitude unveils what life is like in heaven. Indeed, the Beatitudes start and end with dimensions of heaven. And they represent heaven in the context of our life experience here on earth. The greatest fulfillment of our lives is after we die and go to be with Jesus. But we receive a certain first installment of that here. We are a colony of heaven on earth.

The past cannot be forgotten; it
can only be redeemed.

God expects us to represent heaven, not just our traditions, not just our casual, backslid kind of shuffle where we cry out to God when we get into trouble and then stop praying when we get out of trouble. That testimony will not legitimately communicate God's power to the world around us.

He is working to reveal Christ's likeness in us. God is looking for that testimony, the nature of Jesus coming through us. It is reflected in personal healing, character, forgiveness, love, authority, maintaining our peace, walking upright, and having the confidence that "as He is, so are we in this world," as 1 John 4:17 (NKJV) tells us. The Beatitudes unfold with a similar kind of work in us. This is the road map into Christlikeness.

Attitudes dwell in the heart. Ideas dwell in our minds. The Beatitudes are attitudes that God must work in us, not just ideas or concepts but attitudes of the heart. He wants our hearts changed.

And the first of these is, "Blessed are the poor in spirit, for theirs is the kingdom of heaven." What does "poor in spirit" mean? Is Jesus saying that being broke is good, that being poverty-stricken is heavenly? I don't think so. He said, "I came so that they would have life, and have it abundantly" (John 10:10). I don't think He is talking of a physical thing, at least not in this context, that poverty is better than wealth. He is talking about a quality of heart that transcends the physical, that you might have great material possessions but could still be poor in spirit.

Many translations affirm this interpretation of Matthew 5:3. The New English Bible reads, "How blest are those who know their need of God." God's Word says, "Blessed are those who recognize they are spiritually helpless." The New Berkeley translation reads, "Blessed are they who know their spiritual poverty." (See also the New Life Version, the Phillips Revised Student, Edgar Goodspeed's An American Translation, *The Message*, the Wuest Expanded Translation, the New Century Version, and others.)

Consider what Jesus said to the church in Laodicea. He warned, "Because you say, 'I am rich, and have become wealthy, and have no need of anything,' and you do not know that you are wretched, miserable, poor, blind, and naked" (Rev 3:18). The thing that angered the Lord's heart wasn't that they were wretched, miserable, poor, blind, and naked, but that they did not know it. They felt blessed enough to boast that they were "rich...and have no need of anything."

It should frighten us to realize that we can have a religion about God—we might even think everything is fine between God and us—yet be living outside the presence of the Most High and ignorant of our personal need.

God is only as real to us as our need of Him is. The beginning of all spiritual progress is acknowledging our need. Until then we are isolated from God by the stronghold of pride. Remember that God resists the proud but gives grace to the humble. Who are the proud? The proud are those who cannot say, "I have a need."

In our world we do so much to hide from our need. So many of our psychological mechanisms are geared toward keeping us from being honest about our souls' need for righteousness. We are so structured inside that our thoughts automatically justify what we did and why we did it. So then it's difficult for us to look objectively at our need without feeling a sense of condemnation—if we glance at it with any honesty—or to defend ourselves with pride and excuse ourselves for the condition that we're in.

So He says, blessed, happy, and envied are you if you know your need because God's grace is such a perfect shelter that you can look honestly at what you need in light of what God can provide to meet that need. Blessed are you when you know your need.

Our walk with God begins at this point. We begin to see Jesus—who He is, what He can provide, what grace, what power, what example, what virtue can be given to us.

As you begin to define your need, be specific because you can't change until you know what you're changing. You can't ask for the opposite of wrong if you don't know what's wrong in the first place. When God calls us, He takes common people with common problems and says, "I want you to believe in Me and My ability to change you. And here's what I require of you: just be honest about what you need." Try it. The beginning of all spiritual progress starts the moment you discover you have a need and you know specifically what that need is.

If you don't know your need, open your heart and ask the Lord to show you. Our hearts are spring-loaded to the closed position. They are normally closed and guarded. They're normally isolated from hearing the voice of the Lord.

But you can open your heart. Simply pray, "Lord Jesus, I want to know what I need." Then write it down and say, "Lord, I want to repent of it. I renounce it. Lord, I embrace the process of renouncing this thing and the levels it has soaked into my soul year after year. I renounce this."

If two months later the Lord shows you a new level of this thing that's been inside you, don't turn your back on Him. Say, "Lord, go deeper until I'm a reflection of You."

The outcome of God showing you those excessive levels of your need and you repenting of it is not condemnation. The outcome is a greater degree of love. It is such a wonderful thing, because if you're forgiven much, you love much. Your Christianity is only as real as your love is. And you gain love through the forgiveness of your need. Don't be afraid to look at what you are. You can do it.

There's not a person reading this who cannot change, if they are honest with God. No one reading this book needs to be stuck. God can help every single one of us to be a disciple, but there must be a commitment on our part to want to be a disciple. "Jesus, I hear Your voice and want to follow You."

Our hearts are deceitful, but the Lord searches the heart. He gives us the Spirit of truth to show us our own hearts. So when He shows it to you, agree with God and say, "Lord, I want this cleansed. I'm proud, fearful, lustful, judging, anxious (or whatever area it is), and I agree with You, God, and will follow through in my deliverance."

God is as real to you as your need of Him.
You don't really know Him if you don't know
Him as the One who meets your need.

Beloved, just knowing our need is a
significant place of blessedness.

But it begins with saying, "I have a need, Lord Jesus."
The Spirit of truth gives us understanding of who God
is. When the Lord revealed Himself in the Scriptures,
He came as Jehovah Nissi, Jehovah Rapha, and other
names to reveal that God is the answer to anything
we need.

Remember, God is as real to you as your need of
Him. You don't really know Him if you don't know
Him as the One who meets your need.

Beloved, just knowing our need is a significant
place of blessedness. In a world full of self-deception,
where we instinctively blame others for our problems
or are so proud we perceive no wrong within, just
knowing our need is a landmark work of divine grace.
In a world where the heart of man is "deceitful above
all things, and desperately wicked" (Jer. 17:9, KJV), in
heaven's eyes, to tearfully acknowledge our need is a
breakthrough.

JESUS OF THE BIBLE

One may argue, "The Lord I know is loving, not confrontational." Really? I agree He is most loving and accepting of us and has gone to unfathomable lengths to rescue us. Yet that does not mean He is hesitant about correcting us when we are in sin or deception. Consider, to this same church in Laodicea, Jesus described the kind of love He has. He said, "Those whom I love, I rebuke and discipline" (Rev. 3:19).

Personally, I love that Christ confronts me. I love that He shows Himself strong in delivering me from evil. I love that my salvation is not up to me but is the effect of His passionate working in my life. I know He loves me, because He does not leave me to my innate patterns of self-deception.

Again, one argues, "Jesus is the gentle shepherd." Yes, He is. But allow me to illustrate my point with a story.

A while ago I passed through a particularly intense conflict that left me wounded and exhausted. I pleaded with the Lord for an early rescue that didn't come until much later. As I sought Him, He showed me that given the nature of my flesh and the fallen nature of man in general—and considering that the devil was deeply involved in this conflict—Christ had been as gentle as possible with me. But He still confronted me where I was wrong. He still revealed where I fell short. He didn't justify me in the conflict or blame others; He required I repent of where I was incomplete and then forgive those who instigated the conflict. And yet to soothe my wounded soul, He reminded me, "Those whom I [dearly and tenderly] love," the Amplified Bible, Classic Edition says, "I tell their faults and convict and convince and reprove and chasten [I discipline and instruct them]."

If we would be Christ's followers, we must know this about Him. He came that the "thoughts from many hearts may be revealed" (Luke 2:35). Transformational change does not come to us simply because we read biblical doctrines. It comes because Christ reveals our need, and we repent.

Remember what I wrote in chapter 1: the headline of Christ's message is "Repent, for the kingdom of heaven is at hand." His message is not just that we can reach heaven from where we are but that we must also embrace His call to repentance. Beloved, you can attend church for a decade and never inwardly change. Jesus said,

> Many will say to Me on that day, "Lord, Lord, did we not prophesy in Your name, and in Your name cast out demons, and in Your name perform many miracles?" And then I will declare to them, "I never knew you; leave Me, you who practice lawlessness."
>
> —MATTHEW 7:22–23

Jesus is teaching us that seeing our need is the unfolding of His blessing.

I am familiar with those who say, "Jesus always

tells me He loves me." Certainly, no more wonderful
words have ever been spoken in all the universe. But
remember, Christ is the Word of God made flesh. He
was in the beginning with God, and through Him all
things were created. When the Word unites with our
need, Jesus has other things to say in addition to His
love.

> For the word of God is living and active, and
> sharper than any two-edged sword, even pen-
> etrating as far as the division of soul and spirit,
> of both joints and marrow, and able to judge the
> thoughts and intentions of the heart.
>
> —HEBREWS 4:12

Lord, judge our thoughts and the wrongful intentions
of our hearts! The Word is not a doctrine; it's a sword.
It is surgical. It is living. All things are open and laid
bare before the Word—every aspect of our inner man.
He knows what needs repentance, healing, and deliverance. All those things come through our capacity to
hear; in hearing, we discover our need and repent.

From heaven's viewpoint, goodness is not measured
by one's acts of righteousness but by appropriated
righteousness that comes to us from God. *In heaven,
perfection comes in degrees of dependency. It is not a
form of self-attained righteousness but the perfection
of surrender.* And the kingdom of heaven is given to

those who see their need, dismiss the effort to justify themselves, and honestly open their hearts to God.

Our spiritual walk begins when we acknowledge what needs to change. But knowing our need is only the beginning. In the next chapter you will learn that after seeing the need, we must repent, cry to God for change, and let the Lord go deep into our hearts.

> *God, I know that You are not superficially approached. To know the kingdom, I must seek to know Jesus as Lord. I ask You to go deep inside to turn over the fallow ground of my heart. Excavate out of my life all pride, rebellion, lawlessness, fear, lust—any human attitude that has no place in Your kingdom. I surrender it all to You.*

CHAPTER 10

THOSE WHO MOURN

Blessed are those who mourn, for they will be comforted.
—MATTHEW 5:4, NIV

As JESUS CONTINUED training His disciples on the hillside of Galilee, His words began to unfold, layer on layer, awakening the hope that each follower could one day stand clothed in His likeness.

In the first stage of His training, He taught the necessity of recognizing their need—of honestly seeing the sin issues of the heart that would prevent them from ever progressing to Christlikeness.

Now they would discover the critical difference between being taught and being trained in discipleship. He moved them to the second stage with these words: "Blessed are those who mourn, for they will be comforted." The master teacher was about to lay bare the soul, about to begin an excavation that would ultimately expose the root that would bring sorrow, deep mourning, and deep repentance that would get to the core of who they were.

Paul called this process godly sorrow. See what this godly sorrow has produced in you: what earnestness, what eagerness to clear yourselves, what indignation, what alarm, what longing, what concern, what readiness to see justice done. (See 2 Corinthians 7:10.)

THE VOICE OF ONE CRYING

If we are to respond correctly to this second stage of training in Christlikeness, there must be an honest, gut-wrenching repentance that peels back every layer of sin, going deep into our soul to the root of our need.

Only then can Christ change us. God wants to get repentance down to the root of sin.

> Just as it is written in Isaiah the prophet: "Behold, I am sending My messenger before You, who will prepare Your way; the voice of one calling out in the wilderness, 'Prepare the way of the LORD; make His paths straight.'"
>
> —MARK 1:2–3

John the Baptist had this message: prepare the way of the Lord. Make ready a highway for our God.

It wasn't so much that John the Baptist was the one crying in the wilderness; it said he was the *voice* of one crying in the wilderness. "Make ready the way of the Lord." This is something God was saying.

We need to change. We need to be ready for what God wants to do. The first stage is discovering our need and being honest about it. The second stage is where we repent over it; we embrace the sequence, the process of repentance where we say, "I'm sorry." We confess that sin. But then we go on to deal with the strongholds. We examine how those thoughts developed in us before they became attitudes of sin.

An attitude is something that is always there. It's not a fleeting thought, not a bit of information; it's not a new doctrine. It's an attitude of the heart. It's a condition that God works inside us. It becomes the tracks on which the Holy Spirit works, builds, and travels to bring us into Christlikeness.

An attitude of repentance, an attitude of honesty of heart. That's becoming a disciple before Him, and that's what we want.

THE GOAL OF REPENTANCE

The kind of repentance we must have in this second stage of training is far more than just saying, "I'm sorry." That's part of it, but it must go deeper. When John the Baptist baptized the people in a baptism of repentance, the goal was not simply to make them sorry for their sins. The goal of repentance was to make them *ready*. He was showing them how to allow God to work in their hearts to prepare the way for the Lord's coming.

Deep repentance prepares us for
the indwelling presence of the Lord
Jesus Christ, where He is not just
a doctrine, but He is who He is.

Deep repentance prepares us for the indwelling presence of the Lord Jesus Christ, where He is not just a doctrine, but He is who He is. He is the Lord over our lives, and we have fellowship and intimacy with Him. He knows the secrets of our hearts. And we yield our hearts to Him to be dealt with, cleansed, and worked on by Him. And as we share our secrets, He begins to share His secrets. We begin to understand the ways of God and the mysteries of the kingdom of heaven.

When you expose your heart and allow God to deal with areas you have been afraid to acknowledge, God will give you His grace to change and become like Him. Grace is God's enabling power to change. God gives His grace to the man or woman who can say, "God, I need help. Lord, look at this root of need that has kept me from being able to become like You. Change me. I want to change. I must change."

And that beginning is called discipleship. It begins with Christians saying, "I want to be trained; I want to be a disciple. I want to know what I need to know to make a difference in my world so that my roots are strong and my fruit will remain."

God wants to take you through a cleansing process of repentance that excavates deep within your soul and reveals each root of defilement so that you can cast that heavy load of sin on the cross of Christ, so you can live in the power of His resurrection.

In Matthew 3, John the Baptist confronted the Pharisees and Sadducees, warning them that the ax of God's truth was about to cut through their sinful roots and destroy the tree with its fruit of sinfulness. He challenged their hypocritical actions in seeking him to baptize them and boldly told them, "Bring forth fruit that is consistent with repentance [let your lives prove your change of heart]" (Matt. 3:8, AMP).

COMPLETE REPENTANCE

In other words, repentance isn't complete until you start to bring forth the fruit of righteousness. If you've been exhibiting the fruit of selfishness in all you do and say, keep repenting of that selfishness until you are exhibiting the fruit of generosity, and so forth with other areas of sin.

Repentance isn't complete until you start to bring forth the fruit of righteousness.

This discipleship training prepares us to go out and deal with the multitudes who desperately need a Savior at the end of this age. Unless we pass through the excavation of soul that brings us to a place of complete repentance, God cannot entrust us with the power of His kingdom.

Before I was a Christian, I was a hippie. The catch-phrase of my culture was, "If it feels good, do it." Then I became a Christian, and my whole direction turned toward God. I eventually became a pastor. The Lord began to tell me that certain areas of my heart still needed cleansing. I would lay hands on people in prayer, and there was not just Jesus coming through my hands. I could see a filter of Francis there that God wanted to remove.

I wanted to embrace the ministry, and the Lord spoke to my heart severely about what went through my hands. In Hebrew the word *ordain* means to fill the hands. I knew that whatever was in my spirit would be communicated to anyone I laid my hands on.

God began to do this work of cleansing. I went through a time of repentance for that whole lifestyle. For thirty-five to forty days, I was in a process of repentance. It was a sequence of the Lord showing me where certain thoughts first came when I was a young man, what I went through as a teenager, what went through me and stayed there, and how it defiled me.

When I turned to God, I was spiritually born again, but my soul still carried the world's cargo. I had to unload that cargo by confessing it at the cross. As the Lord did this deep work in me, I saw all sorts of things that made me the man I was before I got saved. And every time I saw something, with deep sorrow I asked for forgiveness and cleansing through Jesus' blood.

I've shared this personal story to illustrate that it doesn't matter what our sin is; through repentance and confession, the Lord is able to cleanse areas of our hearts.

God must deal with those areas of our hearts where we are not honest, open, or vulnerable to Him. Becoming honest about our attitude toward sin and embracing the process of pulling down that stronghold requires something more than attending church once a week. It requires a certain aggressiveness in our spiritual walk. We cannot expect everything to be taken care of in the context of a weekly church service.

This second stage in training can be frightening, threatening, and disarming. It can be terrible and wonderful simultaneously because God is working within us—not just some human self-discipline.

The Amplified Bible, Classic Edition helps to clarify this process in Philippians 2:12–13, where it says,

> Therefore, my dear ones...work out (cultivate, carry out to the goal, and fully complete) your own salvation with reverence and awe and trembling....[Not in your own strength] for it is God Who is all the while effectually at work in you [energizing and creating in you the power and desire], both to will and to work for His good pleasure and satisfaction and delight.

We work out what God is working in us. Paul says in 1 Corinthians 12 that there are various ministries but the same Lord. Jesus Christ is working in us. He's the One in charge of bringing ministries into the house of God. He called you to become His disciple, follow Him, and become like Him. And now He's working on you to produce that. It starts with being honest, and it continues into repentance. Repentance is a wholesome and wonderful thing. The kindness of the Lord leads us into repentance. It is good news when God gets ahold of our hearts. It is wonderful when He shows us areas, and we begin to cry and come before Him.

DON'T FEAR THE PROCESS OF REPENTANCE

When we enter this process of repentance by acknowledging our need and allowing God to excavate deep into the soul, laying bare the sinful roots, it awakens a sense of fear in many. For many people, human correction triggers feelings of rejection and being exposed in their failures for all to see. They feel as though someone has blown a whistle and pointed to them, saying, "You are the man...," "You are the woman..." But spiritual correction from a loving God is not rejection. God wants to change us, deliver us, and cleanse us. And it has nothing to do with exposing us before the world.

The moment you come to God to ask for forgiveness of whatever is in your past or present, He forgives you, cleanses you, and then chooses never to remember that sin again. He said, "For I will be merciful and gracious toward their sins and I will remember their deeds of unrighteousness no more" (Heb. 8:12, AMP). That is the wonderful thing about our God.

Years ago in California, a prophet friend of mine was ministering to a Presbyterian pastor and his wife and showed them, by word of knowledge, the inner workings of their hearts. He spoke to them of their past, present, and future, and everything he said was true.

The couple had never seen the gifts of the Spirit operate, and that experience greatly impacted them. They told two more couples, both ministers and their wives, and a few weeks later the two couples attended the service where this prophet was ministering. As he began to minister, he called these four out, had them walk up front, and began speaking to them about their hearts' conditions. He spoke to the first minister, then his wife, then the second minister, and everything he said proved accurate and true.

Then he turned to the second minister's wife, the fourth of the four people that came up, and said to her, "There was a terrible sin in your life." The woman immediately stepped back. You could tell that whatever it was, it was a terrible thing. She looked as if her greatest fear—being exposed in front of the whole church—was about to happen. A hush descended on the congregation because this man knew the secrets of men's hearts, just like John the Baptist.

The prophet said, "There was a terrible sin in your life, and I asked the Lord what it was. And the Lord said, 'I don't remember,' because He had chosen to bury that sin in the sea of His forgetfulness."

That pastor's wife had brought her sin to the Lord repeatedly, never believing His love and grace were big enough or wonderful enough not only to forgive but to put the sin itself out of the reach of God's memory.

She never accepted that she had been genuinely, eternally, completely free from that sin, so the devil constantly beat her up. But then the Lord, in His mercy, stepped into her soul's inner recesses and delivered her from that memory.

So often we struggle with the memory of our need, the ugly sin that used to keep us bound in darkness. We cry out to God, "But God, what about that terrible sin that I used to try to hide? I'm not worthy of Your love and forgiveness to me."

But God lovingly and compassionately looks at us and says, "What sin? I don't remember it!" You see, God has chosen to "take pity on us…and cast all their sins into the depths of the sea" (Mic. 7:19).

Your sin is out of the reach of God's memory because He chose to be forgetful, to remember your sin no more.

That's the God you come to. When you come to repentance and confess your sin, saying, "Lord, I want deliverance from this thing; I want the root taken out; I want an ax laid at the root," you're coming to one who chooses not to hold it against you, who chooses not to spread your sin abroad. You are coming to one who not only will forgive you but will cleanse you of all unrighteousness so that you can stand before God with a clear conscience.

You can look death in the face and say, "You've got nothing on me," because "the sting of death is sin, and the power of sin is the Law," but the blood of Jesus has cleansed you. The enemy can no longer use any weapon to torment or capture your soul. God makes all things new. When you surrender the old to Him, He makes it new. Through repentance, God reaches out to you, lifts you out of the pit of darkness, takes the sin burden off your shoulders, and gives you a new start, a new hope.

The God we serve is not a frowning God with arms folded and finger-pointing. He's a God whose hand is open. I believe you are reading this book because you want to genuinely represent Jesus Christ. I pray God uses these words to do a work inside you. He's getting to those areas that will prove you trustworthy in the days ahead. It will enable Him to give you power because you will not cause others to stumble because of your failures.

When Christ gathered His followers on that hillside of Galilee and said these words: "Blessed are those who mourn, for they will be comforted," He awakened hope in the hearts of those who listened. His words comforted those who had suffered loss or were filled with sorrow over the tragic circumstances of life. God's words speak to us on every level and are activated to comfort us where we need it most.

But those words awakened hope on a much deeper level also. As we pass through this second stage of training in Christlikeness, through supernatural repentance we exchange deep mourning—godly sorrow over our need for forgiveness—for the miraculous hope of receiving God's forgiveness and being transformed from death into eternal life in God's kingdom.

God has a tremendous harvest for the world. But He reaches that harvest by training His people beforehand. Jesus said, "A disciple is not above his teacher," but when he is fully trained, "he may become like his teacher" (Matt. 10:24). Something about being fully trained makes us like Jesus.

If we want to become spiritually mature and grow in the things of God, we must mourn and weep with godly sorrow concerning sin. Without godly sorrow we don't have repentance without regret. We are just always saying we're sorry. The world is full of sorry Christians. We need powerful Christians in this day. We need Christians equipped with weapons of warfare.

Lord, I thank You that I am not disqualified from going through the changes necessary to become what You want me to be. I believe what You say, and I release my faith and commit to paying the price. Work something deep in me so I can bear fruit in keeping with my repentance.

CHAPTER 11

BLESSED ARE THE MEEK

Blessed are the meek, for they will inherit the earth.
—MATTHEW 5:5, NIV

IN THE KINGDOM, there are no great men or women of God, just humble people whom God has chosen to use greatly. How do we know when we are humble? When God speaks, we tremble. God is looking for men and women who tremble at His word. Such people will find the Spirit of God resting on them; they will become a dwelling place for the Almighty.

The divine pursuit begins with the humbling of self. Fleshly desires, soulish fears, and human ambitions try to rule us. Thus, when true meekness emerges in our hearts, it silences the clamor of our fleshly minds. The voice of our fears and inadequacies becomes a whisper. To humble our earthly perspectives and opinions, we must relegate them to a lower priority; they become mere background noise as our focus turns increasingly toward God. No pretense prevails; we come humbling ourselves. We bow on our faces before the holy gaze of God. And in His light, we finally perceive the darkness of our souls.

Thus humility, at its root, starts with honesty. The humbled heart is truly and deeply acquainted with its need, and in the beginning the awareness of one's need becomes the voice of prayer. This confession, "I have sinned," puts us on the side of God concerning it. We agree with our Father that our behavior is wrong. Thus the process of healing begins during this moment of self-discovery. We are working with God to defeat sin in our lives, and in this process of humbling ourselves the Lord grants us peace, covering, and transforming grace.

> In the kingdom, there are no great men
> or women of God, just humble people
> whom God has chosen to use greatly.

Yet with humility we not only acknowledge our need but also take full responsibility for it. We offer no defense to God for our fallen condition. We've come not to explain ourselves but to be cleansed.

The Word says, "Humble yourselves." This means we are choosing it rather than God doing it for us.

> Humble yourselves [with an attitude of repentance and insignificance] in the presence of the Lord, and He will exalt you [He will lift you up, He will give you purpose].
>
> —JAMES 4:10, AMP

There are two ways to enter meekness: humble ourselves or be led through the wilderness. Either path is designed to ultimately lead to a condition of our hearts that will allow us to hear God.

Most of us have gone through times when life's circumstances humbled us. When faced with a difficult situation, we may be humbled, but like a cork in water, we rise back up to the surface, our pride returning when the issue resolves. God doesn't want our lives filled with pride that dissipates during intermittent periods of shame due to external circumstances or even sometimes painful experiences. He wants us to be humble by choice, humble because we want to be like Jesus.

Jesus said, "Come to Me, all you who labor and are heavily burdened, and I will give you rest. Take My yoke upon you, and learn from Me. For I am meek and lowly in heart" (Matt. 11:28–29, MEV). If we want to know the essence of Jesus, we must recognize that He is meek and lowly of heart. He identifies with the lowly. Jesus Christ is humble by choice, by nature. If we will be shaped and conformed to His image, then we too must choose the way of humility and meekness.

THE PATTERN OF MEEKNESS

In this process of spiritual training, God desires to create within us the necessary attitudes that will shape us and condition us to experience the presence of the Lord Jesus Christ in our lives. As we become humble of heart, this step will qualify and prepare us to reach a purity of heart that enables us to see God, have fellowship with Him, and interact spiritually with Him. Then, when He speaks, we will be ready to change, "for it is God Who is all the while effectually at work in you [energizing and creating in you the power and desire], both to will and to work for His good pleasure and satisfaction and delight" (Phil. 2:13, AMPC).

The purpose of the wilderness is not
merely to adjust us to living in a place
of oppression and scarcity; the purpose
of the wilderness is to teach us that
man does not live by bread alone.

God explained this process to the children of Israel in Deuteronomy 8:2–3 (NIV, emphasis added), where He says,

> Remember how the LORD your God led you all the way in the wilderness these forty years, *to humble and test you in order to know what was in your heart, whether or not you would keep his commands.* He humbled you, causing you to hunger and then feeding you with manna, which neither you nor your ancestors had known, to teach you that man does not live on bread alone but on every word that comes from the mouth of the Lord.

The purpose of the wilderness is not merely to adjust us to living in a place of oppression and scarcity; the purpose of the wilderness is to teach us that man does not live by bread alone. In other words, we don't live by our own efforts; the people of God live by every word that proceeds out of the mouth of God.

The goal of this stage of training, this development of the work of humility and meekness in us, is not to make us timid or fearful—it is to give us a humble spirit that can hear the voice of God and follow His leading. The sign of true humility is obedience, trying to live out every utterance, every whisper that comes from God's heart.

The successive stages of spiritual training—recognizing our need, coming through godly sorrow to deep repentance—bring us to true humility of heart and hearing the voice of God speaking to us. The process of God humbling us in the wilderness enables us to hear His voice and be genuinely led by Him.

The Israelites heard the audible voice of God speaking to them from Mount Horeb. The sound of His voice caused great fear in them, and they begged Moses: "Speak to us yourself and we will listen. But do not have God speak to us or we will die" (Exod. 20:19, NIV). Fear is not an aspect of the process of humility that God is working in us in this third stage of training. If fear has awakened in your heart, like the Israelites', you might need more time in the wilderness. Fear or shyness might look like humility, but they are not. How do you know the difference? Fear trembles before *men*. Humility trembles before *God*. The process of meekness and humility will prepare you to hear and receive the word of God with joy and obedience.

THE VOICE OF THE HOLY SPIRIT

God speaks to His followers through the Holy Spirit, and our ability to hear His voice is evidence of our humility. Don't miss that important truth: *our humility is measured by our capacity to hear His voice.* And the way to hear God's voice, the process of coming into that, is acknowledging our need, repenting, and becoming pure in heart. As you continue to embrace that cleansing process, you will become more and more sensitive to the voice of the Holy Spirit.

True humility brings joy when we listen to His voice. His voice may not be audible. The fruit of meekness and humility allows a greater ability to hear the Spirit speaking. Jesus told His followers, "My sheep listen to my voice; I know them, and they follow me" (John 10:27, NIV).

In Psalm 95:7–8 (NIV), David warned the people, "Today, if only you would hear his voice, 'Do not harden your hearts as you did…in the wilderness.'" He is speaking the same words to us: "Today, if you hear his voice, do not harden your hearts" (Heb. 4:7, NIV). A person characterized by humility hears and responds to the voice of the Holy Spirit.

The opposite is also true: if we don't hear the voice of God, it is evidence that we have not embraced the changes God called us into. Eventually we become hypocrites or phony Christians. If we're not changing and going on in the things of God, then we're living with two faces. God wants us to have one face—the face of Christ. He wants us to have one heart—the heart of Christ. He doesn't want us to have duplicity. He wants us to have sincerity of heart, which is one focus, one heart.

A MATTER OF THE HEART

The work of God in this stage of training is to break down areas of resistance. The end of that breaking will result in the characteristic of humility wherein we tremble when God speaks. Through Isaiah the Lord says this:

> These are the ones I look on with favor: those who are humble and contrite in spirit, and who tremble at my word.
>
> —ISAIAH 66:2, NIV

We need hearts that tremble when God speaks, where, when He shows us an area of need, we don't attempt to fight with Him about it or turn away from His voice. In the example of Job, we see a godly man who feared the Lord and was turning away from evil. Of him the Lord said, "Have you considered My servant Job? For there is no one like him on the earth, a blameless and upright man, fearing God and turning away from evil" (Job 2:3).

Just as surely as Job turned away from evil, we can turn away from the voice of the Lord. When the Lord shows us an area of need, our carnal inner man can still turn away, move out of direct communication with God, and choose to do something that prevents us from responding. That's called hardening the heart. Solomon counseled us, "Watch over your heart with all diligence, for from it flow the springs of life" (Prov. 4:23).

God wants to purify our hearts so we can see Him and hear Him speaking to us. He seeks to get to our hearts so that the reality of His presence within can lead us, and He can be the eternal I Am through us. When God's glory returned to the temple in the day of Ezekiel, God spoke to the prophet and said, "Son of man, this is the place of my throne and the place for the soles of my feet" (Ezek. 43:7, NIV). Since the completed work of His Son, Jesus, God is able to dwell within the hearts and souls of man. But just as the Israelites hardened their hearts and turned away from His presence in the temple, we can harden our hearts toward God's voice. When you harden your heart toward God, you soften your heart toward the enemy. When you harden your heart to the voice of God, you are softening your heart to the wicked one.

THE TREMBLING HEART
OF HUMILITY

When God speaks today, He is looking for humility that trembles at the sound of His voice. When we hear His voice, we need to "in humility receive the word implanted, which is able to save your souls" (Jas. 1:21).

When the Word of God comes to us, we don't always immediately obey it. In the second stage of our training—"Blessed are those who mourn"—we learned that we are to work out what God is working in us. Remember, "it is God who works in you to will and to act in order to fulfill his good purpose" (Phil. 2:13, NIV).

There's a time when the word is working in you to will. You haven't attained the goal or fulfilled the work yet, but it's working in you now to will. The enemy sometimes comes to condemn you because you are not fulfilling that word yet. That's when you need humility and to maintain your trembling before God. If we back up one verse, we see that the Word tells us to "continue to work out your salvation with fear and trembling" (Phil. 2:12, NIV). This trembling is humility before the living God, not trembling before men.

Here is where you pray, "Dear Lord, help me to love my enemies, to be pure in spirit, to live free from fear, and in other areas work in me to be willing."

Humility is the initiation of every virtue, every glory, and every increase of Christ in you. You will never get into the future of God's promises without having the humility of God's provision and preparation today.

My friend, I believe with all my heart that you can be equipped. Everyone can pass through these changes to where we carry revival in our souls because God has done the work inside us. None of us is disqualified if we simply believe God and embrace the process of knowing our need, mourning over it, keeping those attitudes of heart, and becoming humble by choice.

DO NOT HARDEN YOUR HEART

It is imperative that you do not harden your hearts at any point along this stairway to Christlikeness. Today you may hear His voice, but if you respond with hardness of heart, it will be harder to hear His voice from this day forward. At first, His voice sounds like one shouting in the wilderness, but if you continue to harden your heart, that voice will be just a whisper in the night until you no longer have the capacity even to hear Him speaking.

Don't harden your heart. God wants to lead you into His presence. The process of training may seem long and daunting, but the only way to Christlikeness is to take each step, one after another.

Think for a moment about the example of David. Samuel anointed David to be the king of Israel when he was just a young shepherd boy. He knew the promise of God for his future, but he was forced to live in the wilderness for years before it came to pass.

Many Christians live in a wilderness where the predators of fear, sin, and futility keep them in caves of darkness until they can embrace their destiny in God. Each of us begins our journey to Christlikeness from a point in the wilderness. As we climb the steps of our training in spiritual maturity, we start the journey from the cave of darkness to the glory of the presence of God. We must embrace this process of change from the inside out.

But until you give yourself over to God's process of change, you will continue to live in a cave of darkness on mountains meant for the presence of God that have been inhabited by the enemy. Guard against hardening your heart so you can progress to Christlikeness. On this third step of your training, God wants you to live a life of humility. You might pray, "O Lord, humble me"—and He can arrange that—but you must choose an attitude of humility through which He can work. These familiar words tell us:

> If my people, who are called by my name, will humble themselves and pray and seek my face and turn from their wicked ways, then I will hear from heaven, and I will forgive their sin and will heal their land.
>
> —2 CHRONICLES 7:14, NIV

You must choose to humble yourself when the voice of God speaks, when the stirring of God is in your inner man, and when He has His finger on some sin from which He wants you to repent. Humble yourself to His voice when you sense some prayer you are supposed to pray, some prophecy you are supposed to give, some dream you are supposed to share. Choose to humble yourself whenever you are supposed to do something.

Make a transition from just humbling yourself during times of adversity and difficulty to becoming a person humble by choice, one who walks with God and hears the voice of God speaking "Be strong and very courageous....Do not turn...to the right or to the left, that you may be successful wherever you go" (Josh 1:7, NIV).

The humility of heart that you choose now will awaken a hunger and thirst for the righteousness of Christ to be evident within you. Choose humility today.

> *Father God, work in me the meekness that*
> *trembles when You speak. Give me a trem-*
> *bling heart, a soft heart, a breaking heart.*
> *Train me to be sensitive to Your Spirit and*
> *to walk in humility before You.*

CHAPTER 12

THOSE WHO HUNGER
AND THIRST

*Blessed are those who hunger and thirst for
righteousness, for they will be filled.*

—Matthew 5:6, NIV

ONE OF THE recurring themes in Scripture is this one question: "What is man that You think of him, and a son of man that You are concerned about him?" (Ps. 8:4). Job voices the same question in a different way when he asks, "What is man that You exalt him, and that You are concerned about him, that You examine him every morning and put him to the test every moment?" (Job 7:17–18). Job was saying, "Why do you deal with me so intensely?"

In another biblical scene David asks this same question. David has passed through the wilderness, past the time of crisis, and is in a time of blessings. As he sings to the Lord, he asks, "When I consider Your heavens, the work of Your fingers, the moon and the stars, which You have set in place; what is man that You think of him, and a son of man that You are concerned about him?" (Ps. 8:3–4).

David continues: "Yet You have made him a little lower than God, and You crown him with glory and majesty!" (v. 5). Some translations of the Bible say, "a little lower than the angels," but the Hebrew word used is *Elohim*, the word used in Genesis 1:1 and most generally used in the Old Testament for "God."[1] Is He saying then that we are a little lower than God?

When God first created man, He planned that man would be an offspring of Himself. Man would have the actual presence of God, and He created man in His likeness.

David was marveling at the creation of God,

including himself, and was filled with awe as he considered it. Perhaps he was sitting and looking at the moon and stars on a bright night. As the morning arose and he saw the dawn with its glory, the colors of the sky emerging in the eastern horizon, he compared their beauty with his own humanity and sang: "When I consider your heavens, the work of your fingers, the moon and the stars, which you have set in place, what is mankind that you are mindful of them, human beings that you care for them?" (Ps. 8:3–4, NIV).

WHAT IS MAN?

What are we? Why does it matter if we obey God? What is the purpose of our existence?

In the beginning, God determined to make man in His image. We read in Ephesians 2:6 that God "raised us up with Him [Christ], and seated us with Him in the heavenly places in Christ Jesus." In Revelation 3:21, Christ confirms that by saying, "The one who overcomes, I will grant to him to sit with Me on My throne, as I also overcame and sat with My Father on His throne."

A time is coming when we will be higher than even the angels in stature, majesty, glory, and authority. But we are not there yet. The Word tells us, "What is man, that You think of him?... You have made him for a little while lower than angels" (Heb. 2:6–7). The angels are not on the throne of God, but God has called His followers to sit with Him in heavenly places. Right now, our position is lower than the angels, but we are going to a higher place. You and I will be in the presence of God. *The promise of life in the presence of God awakens a deep sense of hunger and thirst in our hearts.*

For God's redemptive purposes, we see that we have been humbled to a position lower than the angels, just as Jesus Christ Himself was briefly humbled.

> But we do see Him who was made for a little while lower than the angels, namely, Jesus, because of His suffering death crowned with glory and honor, so that by the grace of God He might taste death for everyone. For it was fitting for Him, for whom are all things, and through whom are all things, in bringing many sons to glory, to perfect the originator of their salvation through sufferings.
>
> —HEBREWS 2:9–10

He is the firstborn, the Son of God, the life giver, and the Word of God incarnate. He grants those who yield their lives to Him the privilege of sitting with Him on His throne. The angels are His army, His worshipping hosts, but we become His bride. In the plan of God, "those who hunger and thirst for righteousness...will be filled" (Matt. 5:6, NIV).

Through the recognition of our need, repentance, and the humbling of our hearts, as we begin to hear the voice of God speaking within us, a reality awakens deep hunger and thirst for the fulfillment of the purposes of God. We begin to tremble at the promise as we contemplate, "Is this what I am? Was this what man was created to be?" *We begin to see that humanity has been created in the image and likeness of God.*

For a little while, we are lower than the angels. But right now, we are in the process of change, which begins with honesty. Honesty leads to repentance, and then as we become humble and meek, we experience a hunger and thirst for the righteousness of God.

We hear what God has been after all along. It is not just to leave sin so we can have a comfortable existence; it's to obtain righteousness. And the righteousness that we are talking about looks glorious. It is the fullness of glory.

This hunger and thirst that we experience awaken a deep longing for righteousness. It is like a hidden treasure that, once found, gives joy. "The kingdom of heaven is like a treasure hidden in a field, which a man found and hid; and for joy over it he goes and sells all that he has and buys that field" (Matt 13:44, NKJV). Our pursuit of it is "like a merchant seeking beautiful pearls, who, when he had found one pearl of great price, went and sold all that he had and bought it" (Matt. 13:45, NKJV).

POSSESSING THE TREASURE

In the previous verse, the treasure was hidden under dirt. To get to the treasure, you must get the dirt off. Our lives inside are full of dirt and things that need to be cleansed, but underneath that dirt is the hidden treasure. That treasure is Christ in you, the hope of glory.

When we can see the treasure, our hunger and thirst for the righteousness of Christ compel us to sell everything and cast out anything that could hide that treasure. You might not be able to see the treasure yet. It's not open, not visible, but remember, the promise of God to you is: "The one who overcomes, I will grant to him to sit with Me on My throne, as I also overcame and sat with My Father on His throne" (Rev. 3:21).

God has no people who started out perfect;
He has only people whom He has changed.

We have all felt disqualified by our imperfections because we identified more with our sins than God's promise. Everyone He's ever used has had to overcome their need and stay repentant. God has no one who started out perfect; He has only people whom He has changed. They were honest, and they became meek. They began to hunger and thirst for righteousness' sake. They overcame and became people God used.

As you are filled with a deep hunger and thirst for more of God, allow the power of the Holy Spirit to stir you into action, into walking with God. No one is disqualified from being filled with God's righteousness once they take these steps into Christlikeness, overcoming anything that would hold them back. Male, female, young or old, it means nothing. The character of the heart is everything as far as the dealings of God go. Nothing less than Christlikeness will do, but Christ, "by the power that enables him to bring everything under his control, will transform our lowly bodies so that they will be like his glorious body" (Phil. 3:21, NIV).

That's where we are going. It is why we hunger and thirst and embrace the changes God has set before us. The deep longing within us will propel us through the changes required of our souls. Like Jesus, who "for the joy set before him...endured the cross, scorning its shame, and sat down at the right hand of the throne of God" (Heb. 12:2, NIV), we will continue in the process until we experience the joy of the presence of God within our hearts. Like the example in Proverbs, "the appetite of laborers works for them; their hunger drives them on" (Prov. 16:26, NIV).

I have a hunger to reach my destiny in God. I have a passion for becoming what God wants me to be. I don't want the blessing of God to allow me to stay the way I am; I want my life to be changed and transformed. He must go in and remove self out of the way. God will not pour new wine into old wineskins.

The more your heart has been freed of selfishness, the deeper the excavation of your soul through repenting of pride, the more your spirit will become honest and truthful before the Lord, and the more you will hear the promise of God over your life. *You have been called and are being prepared for a visitation from God and to become a habitation of God, "in whom you also are being built together into a dwelling of God in the Spirit" (Eph. 2:22).*

ARE YOU HUNGERING AND THIRSTING?

Being the habitation of God is a spiritual reality for every follower of Christ. It is your destination. There must be a constant hunger and thirst within, not just on a Sunday morning or in scattered moments throughout your day. You have been called to be a disciple—in your workplace, school, environment, neighborhood, and home.

To be a disciple, you must allow your hunger and thirst for righteousness to keep you moving forward in God until you get to the throne of God. That's the goal for your hunger and thirst. A young man came to a sage, a wise old man, and said, "I want to know God. Tell me how to truly know God."

The wise old man replied, "You want to know about God? Do you want to know who God is? Come with me." He walked down a hill to a lake, then walked right into the lake.

The young man thought, "I'm going to be baptized. He will do something here."

The wise man turned around as the young man walked into the water. The young man was about neck deep, and the older man put his hand on the young man's head and put him under the water. The young man thought, "He's baptizing me; he'll let me up in a minute."

But the old man didn't let him up. He held him down. He continued to hold him under the water until the young man's lungs were ready to burst because he was drowning. Finally, he pushed the old man's arms off and burst through the water. His face was startled and shocked.

The old man said, "When you want God the way you wanted air, you'll understand the hunger and thirst necessary to bring you into the presence of God."

> As the deer pants for the water brooks, so my soul pants for You, God. My soul thirsts for God, for the living God; when shall I come and appear before God?
>
> —PSALM 42:1–2

What are hunger and thirst? They are emptiness. That is what the beginning stage of our journey has been producing: emptiness. You have been emptied of pride, self, and ambition. God has been excavating the dirt out of His building site in your heart. The mighty shovel of God's hand can remove all fears and sins, making us a fearless, holy people before Him. Through Him, nothing is impossible. And it can happen for everyone, including you.

Perhaps you feel that God has never used you for anything. Maybe you have been tucked so deeply into obscurity that you have never peeked out to see what life was about, afraid to live and afraid to die.

Allow me to encourage you to get out. Get involved in the process. Get involved in repentance. Get involved in being honest before God. Get involved in becoming meek and trembling when God speaks. Embrace this process of change.

> *Lord, show me that the way of change is the way of honesty, repentance, and humility, leading to hunger, hearing, and seeing God. Lord, give me faith to believe that You're bigger than my excuses for why I can't change. Deal with my sin and get to the heart of the matter so that You can reveal Yourself. Help me embrace the call to be a disciple of Jesus Christ.*

CHAPTER 13

BLESSED ARE THE MERCIFUL

Blessed are the merciful, for they will be shown mercy.
—MATTHEW 5:7, NIV

THUS FAR IN our journey to spiritual maturity, we have uncovered vital characteristics that create a road map for Christians who want more of God. These characteristics of a repentant and humble heart and a spirit vulnerable to the voice of God—one filled with a deep hunger and thirst for the righteousness of God—are what heaven looks like.

> The biggest obstacle to being used by God in our society is not the devil. It's not the world or a political party. Perhaps it is the hearts of self-satisfied Christians who are proud, are unrepentant of their own sins, and will not give themselves to the process of change. They are angry about the condition of the world while being totally ignorant of the condition of their own hearts.

For those who have experienced the deep hunger and thirst for the righteousness of God that we saw in the previous chapter, the next step in the sequence is now experiencing God's awesome, supernatural mercy. Though we hunger and thirst for righteousness, we still stumble with unmerciful attitudes at times. How do we get more mercy?

The biggest obstacle to being used by God in our society is not the devil. It's not the world or a political party. Perhaps it is the hearts of self-satisfied

Christians who are proud, are unrepentant of their own sins, and will not give themselves to the process of change. They are angry about the condition of the world while being totally ignorant of the condition of their own hearts.

The world needs to see Christians who can admit when they're wrong, who can humble themselves and get close enough to God to make a difference in the scene around them. God wants people born of Him, with the light of Jesus Christ coming through them.

GOD WANTS A PERFECT CHURCH

Many of us know how to be religious but not merciful. How do we learn to be constantly forgiving, always ready to go the extra mile, turn the other cheek, and give away our cloak when someone asks for our shirt—all the next-level attributes God calls us to in our walk with Him? When everything inside us has bent to our being selfish, protective, and me-first inclined, how do we make the transformation to being merciful?

To fully understand what becoming merciful means, we must recognize that God's standard for the church is perfection. Most of God's followers fail to recognize God's seriousness in calling His body to be perfect.

In His Sermon on the Mount, Jesus taught, "Be perfect, therefore, as your heavenly Father is perfect" (Matt. 5:48, NIV). That's the standard God calls the church to be. Paul expanded on this by saying, "And

He gave some to be apostles, some prophets, some evangelists, and some pastors and teachers, for the equipping of the saints for the work of ministry, for the edifying of the body of Christ, till we all come to the unity of the faith and of the knowledge of the Son of God, to a perfect man, to the measure of the stature of the fullness of Christ" (Eph. 4:11–13, NKJV).

When speaking of believers as the bride of Christ, Paul taught that Christ washes us with water through the Word so that we might be "a radiant church, without stain or wrinkle or any other blemish, but holy and blameless" (Eph. 5:27, NIV). God's standard is ever present to be a perfect standard. The Lord does nothing sloppy or halfway. He doesn't say, "OK, I want you to love on Mondays, Wednesdays, and Fridays, but you can slack off the rest of the week."

That's not God. Looking at the Bible, you will repeatedly see that God's standard for the church is perfection. You might be wondering why I'm repeating this point. It's simple: *if we do not understand God's standard, we will tolerate all sorts of imperfections within us.*

In chapters 2 and 3 of the Book of Revelation, Jesus spoke to the churches. He required every one of them to be holy and blameless in an evil world. He said, "I know where you live—where Satan has his throne" (Rev. 2:13, NIV). That's a bold statement!

I don't know what spiritual battles they were facing, but He required them to walk uprightly.

- He said to the church at Ephesus, "You have forsaken the love you had at first. Consider how far you have fallen" (vv. 4–5, NIV).

- He said to the church at Pergamum, "There are some among you who hold to the teaching of Balaam, who taught Balak to entice the Israelites to sin" (v. 14, NIV).

- He said to the church at Thyatira, "You tolerate that woman Jezebel" (v. 20, NIV).

- He said to the church at Sardis, "You have a reputation for being alive, but you are dead....I have found your deeds unfinished" (Rev. 3:1–2, NIV).

- He said to the church at Laodicea, "You are lukewarm—neither hot nor cold—I am about to spit you out of my mouth" (v. 16, NIV).

- Even to the churches of Smyrna and Philadelphia, which did not receive His rebuke, He counseled, "Be faithful, even to the point of death....Hold on to what you have, so that no one will take your crown" (Rev. 2:10; 3:11, NIV).

He spoke to them exactly what they needed in the context of the world around them.

MERCY TRIUMPHS OVER JUDGMENT

To think that God requires less than perfection is to take the deity of God, the perfection of God, and try to reduce it to some human understanding of who God is.

How can you ever measure up to God's standard of perfection? You will make real progress at becoming merciful only by seeing who Christ is and recognizing where you are in light of His perfection and mercy.

Let me explain how it works in my life. Initially, we don't realize how hard this is because we are still comparing ourselves with other Christians. But then God begins to deal with us about pride and judging others, and He shows us areas of our need. We begin to see the size of that standard.

At this point, we are forced to decide. We can either begin to humble ourselves and admit we have fallen short of Christ's standard for the church, or become Christian pharisees, meaning we become self-righteous and avoid dealing with issues of the heart.

Begin by embracing one change at a time. Some changes will happen quickly; others will take time and persistence. Some areas of our souls will not go down without a fight. They won't be as easy to change.

GOD'S MERCY

What can you do when you realize that you've been keeping God's standard in some areas, but in others you've fallen short? You come to God and say, "Oh, God, I've blown it. I get so angry when this person treats me this way. This is the fifteenth time today I blew it. God, I need Your help. Please forgive me."

God begins to show you His unfailing mercy in those moments of deep honesty and need. He says, "I know that you have blown it again today. I watched you try to change and fail to make the change and do it again. I know that you are struggling, but you are trying. So I will make a deal with you. I will give you grace because you are humbling yourself. But I won't forgive this one."

"Wait! What?" you cry out to Him. "Well, then, what can I do about this, God?"

"If you want Me to forgive you, you must forgive your neighbor. I will not forgive you until you forgive the person you can't stand." The Bible calls this the law of liberty.

> So speak and so do as those who will be judged by the law of liberty. For judgment is without mercy to the one who has shown no mercy. Mercy triumphs over judgment.
> —JAMES 2:12–13, NKJV

Do you have someone in your life like that? Who comes to mind as you read this? The person at work you're hoping has a long vacation or gets fired? That nosy neighbor who always wants to know your business? Maybe it is several people. They seem to be there to antagonize you.

God says, "I want you to forgive the person you can't stand."

"Oh, God," you cry, "can't we make this a multiple choice? What are options B and C?"

We will not obtain mercy unless we are first merciful. We have no other options.

Jesus said, "Forgive us our debts as we also have forgiven our debtors" (Matt. 6:12, NIV). He said, "Blessed are the merciful, for they shall receive mercy." Then, to make sure we would get the point, in Matthew 18, He told a parable about a man who had millions of dollars' worth of debt and could only be forgiven if he forgave the man who owed him.

The Word tells us: "Forgive him, that your Father in heaven may also forgive you your trespasses" (Mark 11:25, NKJV). We will not obtain mercy unless we are first merciful. We have no other options.

Desperate for the mercy of God, you begin to show mercy to others, beginning by forgiving the person who causes you so much grief. In your first wobbly steps toward forgiving others, you are motivated only by your desire to have peace with God, because you desperately want His forgiveness.

"All right, Lord, if I can't have complete openness in my fellowship with You unless I forgive, then I forgive this person." Your motives aren't virtuous, but you're trying to move in the right direction. And the moment you do that, something happens inside you. That area contained by your deep need for self-preservation and self-righteousness begins to yield to God, and a little bit of mercy goes out. You take a step closer to that standard of God's perfection.

YOU GET WHAT YOU GIVE

The way that God operates is by giving to you what you give to others. You get what you give. You give a little bit of mercy, and a little bit of mercy comes to you. So you give a little more mercy, a little bit more grace. You begin to forgive that person. Eventually, you start thinking that person changed because they no longer antagonize you. You don't see what's happening in you. God's goal in giving you mercy only when you give it first was to move you upward toward His standard of perfection.

The goal of Christian perfection is not some
strict little law or line we are to walk on,
one foot after the other. The perfection
of a Christian is the perfection of love.

109

Jesus tells us, "Be perfect, therefore, as your heavenly Father is perfect" (Matt. 5:48, NIV). Luke expands the meaning of those words for us by saying, "Be merciful, just as your Father is merciful" (Luke 6:36, NIV). The goal of Christian perfection is not some strict little law or line we are to walk on, one foot after the other. *The perfection of a Christian is the perfection of love.*

God uses our sin to stimulate love. We weren't focusing on the love part while trying to deal with the sin issue. But while we were honestly dealing with our sin, love was beginning to increase, helping us deal with the areas of sin in our lives. And as love continues to increase, we give more of the forgiveness that God requires us to give.

Ultimately, we can fulfill that standard of perfection, which is a standard of mercy. God gives us a biblical example to help us understand this process in Luke 7. Jesus went to dinner in the home of a Pharisee. As they sat to eat, a woman followed Jesus in, knelt at His feet, and began to wash His feet with her tears, wiping them with her hair. Simon, the Pharisee who invited Jesus to dinner, knew this woman was a prostitute and said to himself: "If this man were a prophet, he would know who is touching him and what kind of woman she is—that she is a sinner" (Luke 7:39).

Jesus read Simon's mind and said,

> Do you see this woman? I came into your house.
> You did not give me any water for my feet, but

she wet my feet with her tears and wiped them
with her hair. You did not give me a kiss, but
this woman, from the time I entered, has not
stopped kissing my feet. You did not put oil on
my head, but she has poured perfume on my
feet. Therefore, I tell you, her many sins have
been forgiven—as her great love has shown. But
whoever has been forgiven little, loves little.

—LUKE 7:44–47, NIV

When you begin to make the changes necessary to
meet God's standard, you start to realize how much
you have been forgiven. Jesus said if you've been forgiven little, you love little. The converse is also true:
if you've been forgiven much, you love much. As you
begin to absorb the mercies of God, you realize that
you have been forgiven of much. And in the process
of His mercies flowing into your life, they begin to
flow out to others. The consequence of seeing your
need in light of God's standard is a love that loves
much. That is the wonder of God's ways. "We love
because He first loved us."

God's standard is not a law, a religion that you must
hold to. It isn't a religious regimen; it's a walk with
God. God provides the standard through Jesus Christ
Himself. In the process of our recognizing our need
to change, seeing how much we need the mercy of
God, He produces a repentance that gives us His gift

of mercy as we learn to let mercy flow out of our lives into the lives of others.

PEOPLE WHO LOVE MUCH

The outcome of this process of excavation and humbling ourselves before God is not an oppressed people but a people who love much. Our world, cities, and neighborhoods need people who love much, instead of those Christians I mentioned before who are angry about the condition of the world but ignorant about the condition of their own hearts.

If we intend to be the people God wants us to be, then we must be people who reveal Jesus in His mercy. "Blessed are the merciful." God's kind of mercy is not inherent within us until we find that mercy at the throne of God and begin to exercise the process of giving that mercy out.

You will find people around you who are the most annoying, unsanctified people in your life—but in the hands of God they could be divinely appointed people. I want you to see that they are in your life to perfect love in you.

God is thrusting you into a place where you will have to draw on His grace for your own need. He wants you to use the love that you receive from Him to meet their need. You might not win that person you are learning to love, but God wants you to know that you will win a harvest in the relationships around you when they see your love in an unjust situation. They will see your mercy, your forgiveness, your giving out of the life of God.

The world is looking for Christians who, in the conflicts of life, reveal Jesus. You are one of them; you are it! Ask the Lord to fill you with His mercy. Be a disciple of Christ who is baptized in the mercy and love of God, one who is determined to pass through all the spiritual conditions of heart that will lead you to exhibit Christlikeness.

> *Lord, help me to become merciful toward my neighbors, my spouse, and my children. I want to be a mercy-motivated person— not because I want my own needs met but because I want to see more of Your heart. You are love, and Your plan from the beginning has been to make me in Your image. My chief desire is to see Your heart and know you more.*

CHAPTER 14

THE PURE IN HEART SEE GOD

Blessed are the pure in heart, for they will see God.
—MATTHEW 5:8, NIV

THE WHOLE OF the mystery of our existence is centered in perfecting the conditions of the heart. It certainly is possible to be successful on some human level, being fulfilled in all the horizontal relationships that surround us and flow in and out of our lives. But the divine reason we exist is so that God can get to our hearts. In earlier stages of this spiritual training, we have learned that the trembling heart, the humbled heart, the honest heart is the beginning of change.

But God is after something more. The heart is the seat of reality—the reality that God looks at. God doesn't look at the outer appearance; He looks on the heart and sees things you think you've secretly hidden away where no one sees them. He says: "Who can hide in secret places so that I cannot see them?" (Jer. 23:24, NIV). All things are laid bare before His eyes, and His word is "alive and active. Sharper than any double-edged sword, it penetrates even to dividing soul and spirit, joints and marrow; it judges the thoughts and attitudes of the heart" (Heb. 4:12, NIV).

God is after your heart. Jesus said, "For out of the heart come evil thoughts—murder, adultery, sexual immorality, theft, false testimony, slander" (Matt. 15:19, NIV). God wants the condition of the heart to be right. The mystery of our existence is unlocked through the perfecting of our hearts through Christ's indwelling Spirit.

Often the focus of all our efforts is on finding

satisfaction in life. We want to have fulfillment and to see our earthly dreams come to pass. Yet all these things will pass away, while the condition of your heart will endure forever.

The mystery of our existence is unlocked through the perfecting of our hearts through Christ's indwelling Spirit.

Revelation 22:4 reveals that there will be a point in time when the reward of heaven for the disciples of Christ will be "they will see His face." But if our focus today is on seeing the fulfillment of our earthly dreams instead of being consumed with a passion and desire to see the face of God, to know God daily, then we are not exhibiting the characteristics of those who are pure in heart. Unless our passion to know Christ is urging us on in our daily endeavors spiritually, we have become too preoccupied and distracted with the things of this age. We have been dissipated, deceived, and drained of our lives' purpose.

God desires intimacy with us. To seek His face is to behold the divine expression and hear the tone of His voice. From the vantage point of His presence, we can turn from evil. For to know His love is to know why we've been created.

PERFECTED FOR THE PLEASURE OF GOD

Life has been given to you to perfect you for God's pleasure. That's the reason you exist. You don't exist for your own ends, your own pleasure. If you think you do, you have been deceived by the enemy of your soul.

What does it mean to become Christlike? It means we choose to live for one purpose: to give pleasure to God. To accomplish this, we must be intimately acquainted with that in which His soul delights. Jesus always chose to give God pleasure, even amid conflict and cruelty. Thus, when injustice wounds us, we must redeem our experiences with mercy. Let us make the Sermon on the Mount our standard of conduct. Let us discover those ways that will reveal Christ through us and thus bring pleasure to God.

As it is written:

> Thou art worthy, O Lord, to receive glory and honour and power: for thou has created all things, and for thy pleasure they are and were created.
>
> —REVELATION 4:11, KJV

The key to lasting happiness and true fulfillment in this world is not found in self-gratification but in bringing gratification to the heart of God. And while the Lord desires that we enjoy His many gifts, He wants us to know that we are created not only by Him but for Him as well.

So God works on the heart. He penetrates the heart and deals with our defenses. He breaks down walls, sweeps in, and does whatever is necessary to get to our heart. God is after your heart because the pure in heart will see God—not just in eternity but now!

You will begin to see God as He emerges in the church. As you begin to see Him, you will see what He wants to do in the earth. You start to rise above the fears in your heart. You rise above the competition, ambition, lusts, and self-desires. As you repent of them and get cleansed, your heart is purified and you see God.

God is adding the attribute of purity of heart to those attributes you have been acquiring. God will work that attitude into those who become the merciful, who hunger and thirst for righteousness, who are meek by choice, who mourn before Him and know their need. The outcome of this sequence is to see God, to perceive God.

Jesus said, "Where your treasure is, there your heart will be also" (Matt. 6:21, NIV). What is your treasure? What is it that you are always thinking about? What occupies your mind? Your treasure is there.

Some of our treasures are just earthly, depressing things. Our hearts often dwell on our fears, problems, or things in the past. Those things become our treasure, and that can be an idolatrous thing. Do you understand why God wants to deliver us? It is because so often we don't even know the difference between the wonderful treasure of a pure heart and the overwhelming cares of our earthly treasures. "Blessed are the pure in heart....They will see God."

When Jesus worked miracles, how did He do those miracles? Was there some inherent power inside humanity that He tapped into? Not in any way. Acts 10:38 says, "God anointed Him with the Holy Spirit and with power, and how He went about doing good and healing all who were oppressed by the devil, for God was with Him."

Jesus did the miracles because He was pure in heart and saw the Father. He did only the things He saw the Father do. The people got healed because the Father was healing. The waterfall of God's presence was about to heal someone, and Jesus, seeing what the Father was doing, and being empowered by the Holy Spirit, stepped into God's presence and stretched forth His hands. He touched those in need, and they were healed.

Jesus tells us, "If anyone...does not doubt in their heart but believes what they say will happen, it will be done for them" (Mark 11:23, NIV). Why? How can you not doubt in your heart?

Well, if you see God doing it, you will not doubt in your heart. But if you are just doing it yourself, you will have days when you doubt. You will have times when you wonder, "Is this me or God?" But if your heart is pure and the Lord has spoken to you, confirmed it, and burned it in you, and you know it is God, then you won't doubt in your heart.

The way to the miracle power of God is becoming pure in heart. These people look through the creation of the world, and they see God. They are in touch with the real God. They have fellowship with God, and their eyes behold him. And because they see Him and hear Him, they do what He does. They say what He says.

Where is our treasure? Do we long to see Him? Do we think about someday coming before His throne, beholding His glory, myriads of angels, and the redeemed standing in awe of Him? And there He is, the source of life and the universe.

That passion, I believe, compelled the first-century saints. They yearned for that day when they would leave this world, where they had been persecuted and fought for survival. They weren't invested in earthly things. Their investment was in heaven because the enemy surrounded them on earth. But we have a comfortable life, drowning in things. We are rooted and grounded here in emptiness. This world gets ahold of us, and it's why our hearts must be purified.

THE PURE IN HEART SEE GOD

God's purification process cleanses the condition of our hearts and opens our eyes. Jesus warned that the

Pharisees were blind leaders of the blind. Jesus wants us to see where we are going. The Scripture says, "Thou wilt shew me the path of life: in thy presence is fulness of joy; at thy right hand there are pleasures for evermore" (Ps. 16:11, KJV). The pleasures of this world are a dim reflection of the pleasures of eternity. But seeing eternity is not our main objective. We must aim to see the One who made it and live in fellowship with Him.

He did reveal Himself to people in the Scriptures, and they witnessed the glory of God—He revealed Himself to Isaiah, Abraham, Ezekiel, Jeremiah, Solomon, David, and Habakkuk. God also revealed Himself to Peter, James, and John on the mountain.

The Son of God is the mediator between God and man. Jesus Christ, who carries the glory of the Father, is the only One who has ever directly revealed Him.

Beloved, to see Jesus is to behold God. But first, we must renounce every perception of the Almighty other than what we have found proved true in Christ.

Therefore, study the life, teachings, and deeds of Jesus Christ, and you will remove the veil of mystery surrounding the nature of God.

Jesus said, "He who has seen Me has seen the Father" (John 14:9, NKJV).

What truth could be more profound? Each time we read what Jesus did, we behold the nature of God. Every time we listen to what Jesus taught, we hear the voice of the living God.

Jesus is the image of the invisible Father (Heb. 1:2–3). He mirrored on earth those things He saw His Father doing in heaven; He echoed the words the Father whispered to Him from eternity.

Do you truly desire to see God? Christ's words are windows through which the pure in heart behold the Almighty.

> God, after He spoke long ago to the fathers in the prophets in many portions and in many ways, in these last days has spoken to us in His Son.
>
> —HEBREWS 1:1–2

The teachings of Jesus Christ are not to be blended into the Scriptures as though He were one of many equally important voices used by God. He is, in truth, the living revelation of God Himself, the sole expression of His invisible glory.

- Prophets point the way; Christ is the way.

- Teachers expound on the truth; Jesus is the truth.

- Apostles proclaim the life; Jesus is the life.

- Yes, all speak the Word, but the Son of God is the Word.

When Christ speaks, we are listening to God unfiltered, unbiased, and unveiled.

BLESSED ARE THE PURE IN HEART

Jesus said the pure in heart would see God. David wrote, "To the pure you show yourself pure" (2 Sam. 22:27). Think about it, not only can we truly know God, but also He desires to show Himself to us.

His promise is not reserved for a time later in heaven, but in some deep measure, He desires to fulfill His words here and now.

We might have grown content with the illusion of distance, yet God is not content. He created us to live in steadfast union with His presence. The sense of distance between the Almighty and ourselves is a deception.

Indeed, the Lord corrects us not merely because He hates sin but because sin separates us from His presence. He loves us and purifies us so we can see Him.

The church has gotten so conditioned by the lack of God's presence that the lack of God has become "orthodox Christianity." We have made a closed heaven normal.

God seeks to open the heavens and be God to us. He is already in our midst, but we sometimes fail to recognize Him. We're the same as those two men walking the road to Emmaus. Jesus asked them, "What happened today?" They filled Him in without ever recognizing Him. They were telling Jesus about Jesus. He opened the Scriptures to them. But they didn't see Him because it wasn't revealed to them. (See Luke 24:15–17.)

Then later, as He was breaking bread, it says that

He was revealed, their eyes were opened, they saw He was the Son of God, and then He vanished from their sight. They said, "Were not our hearts burning within us?" (Luke 24:32, NIV).

Once Jesus is revealed, it impacts the heart. If God is touching your heart, God is purifying you for Himself. Ask God to give you an enterable heart so that He can whisper, "This is the way," whenever you turn to the right or the left (Isa. 30:21).

Remember, the whole reason for our existence is the perfection of our hearts. Everything, even the way you look, is constantly changing. It's not in how you appear before people—how you dress or what you do. It's what you are before God. Everything else will be swept away. But where your heart is, there your treasure is. Proverbs 4:23, NKJV, says, "Keep your heart with all diligence, for out of it spring the issues of life."

The pure in heart see God, and it's God in them that enables them to see God in others. God is among us. I believe He wants to lead us to a place where our minds are filled with His glory. Something changes inside us when we begin to see God.

The problem with the disciples is that they didn't see Him. If you look at John 14:8, the disciples said, "Lord, show us the Father, and it is enough for us." And Jesus said, "Have I been with you so long and still you don't know Me?" He said, "He who has seen Me has seen the Father." We think that with that kind of statement, the next verse would read, "And they all fell on their faces and trembled." But they didn't. Instead, they all just sat there. "What do you mean, if I see You, I see the Father?" They couldn't grasp that God was in Christ, reconciling the world to Himself.

The Bible also says in Luke 10:21,

> At that very time He rejoiced greatly in the Holy Spirit, and said, "I praise You, Father, Lord of heaven and earth, that You have hidden these things from the wise and intelligent and have revealed them to infants. Yes, Father, for doing so was well pleasing in Your sight. All things have been handed over to Me by My Father, and no one knows who the Son is except the Father, and who the Father is except the Son, and anyone to whom the Son determines to reveal Him."

John 14:6 says, "I am the way, and the truth, and the life; no one comes to the Father except through me."

Jesus said the revealed knowledge of the Father comes only to those to whom the Son wills to reveal Him, and He reveals the glory of God only to babes. Little children are pure in heart.

Oh, Lord Jesus, help me become aware of my heart's condition. Help me live sensitively in my inner man, vulnerable to Your voice, so that You can purify me with your Word.

Lord, help me love it when You chasten me. You're making me pure. You're enabling me to become capable of seeing You.

CHAPTER 15

PEACEMAKERS

*Blessed are the peacemakers, for they
will be called children of God.*

—MATTHEW 5:9, NIV

THE NEXT PHASE is becoming a peacemaker. In the Sermon on the Mount, Jesus said peacemakers are called the children of God. Jesus speaks about a current stature of sonship that the church is to embrace. Not fast-forwarding beyond what is written or what is possible to attain in this life but what the Bible calls sonship. And the sequence of spiritual maturity—repentance, humbling our hearts, hungering for righteousness, becoming merciful and pure in heart—all the preparation leads us to a place where we are beginning to see God, and as we see God, we begin to become sons of God.

God has been after this since the beginning of time. "Then God said, 'Let Us make man in Our image, according to Our likeness.'...In the image of God He created him, male and female He created them" (Gen. 1:26–27, NKJV). When I write about sons of God, this is not a gender term; it's a spiritual term. These are allegorical terms representing a certain relationship that we have with God. A son is one who has been begotten, trained, and whom the father has poured his life into. Those who are sons of God are led by the Spirit of God. But to be led by the Spirit of God, you've got to see God. All this is a sequence of God bringing us into a spiritual place of maturity that the Bible calls sonship.

Adam was the first son of God. Perhaps you have been raised without a living, interactive father or in a home where your natural father wasn't present. I want to tell you that there's a Father in heaven who can make up for whatever imperfect parenting has occurred in your life. All of us earthly fathers are imperfect. Whatever the degree of lack, there's a supply of grace from God the Father. He says in Isaiah 45:11 (NKJV), "Thus says the LORD, the Holy One of Israel, and his Maker: 'Ask Me of things to come concerning My sons; and concerning the work of My hands, you command Me.'"

If you look at the genealogy of Jesus in the Book of Luke, it rewinds back to Adam. In the beginning, God created man. Man fell. Still, God's work prevails.

The Word says that the kindness of God leads us to repentance (Rom. 2:4). So, when you begin to repent, that's the work of God's hand. When you learn to be humble and hear the truth of God's Word, that's the work of God's hand. "This is the work of God, that you believe in Him whom He sent" (John 6:29). Nobody can come to the Son except the Father draw Him. That's a work of God that has been going on in your life even to this moment.

God is working on you. Not religion. Not the church, but the real God. He's working on you, and He says that you can ask Him concerning His children, and every time you ask Him about them, you can commit to Him the work of His hands.

Thus says the Lord, The Holy One of Israel, and his Maker: "Ask Me of things to come concerning My sons; and concerning the work of

My hands, you command Me. I have made the
earth and created man on it. I—My hands—
stretched out the heavens, and all their host I
have commanded."
—ISAIAH 45:11–12, NKJV

Whatever your thoughts are about being a spiritual son or daughter of God, it will be more than your
expectations.

When you follow the sequence of the Beatitudes,
it leads to a kind of life people in this world don't
know about. It's a work from God that shapes the
container of your soul so that you receive a blessing
like heaven in its substance and character. This has
been God's plan from the beginning, to make man
and woman in the image of His Son.

Look at Romans 9:23 (NKJV). He says, "That He
might make known the riches of His glory on the ves-
sels of mercy, which He had prepared beforehand for
glory." God is doing this; He's preparing us for glory.
This whole time is a time of preparation and not just
for salvation. We define *salvation* as just coming out of
the region of hell, but it's coming into the glory of God.

The Word of God says, "Come out from among them
and be separate, says the Lord. Do not touch what is
unclean" (2 Cor. 6:17, NKJV). "I will walk among you
and be your God, and you shall be My people" (Lev.
26:12, NKJV). "And you shall be My sons and daughters" (2 Cor. 6:18, NKJV).

Blessed are the peacemakers, for they shall be called sons of God. You can't be a peacemaker if you don't know the Prince of Peace who abides in you. You have peace because you know who is in charge of your life. You experience the power of knowing why you exist.

You begin to see God. Because once you see God, you are more aware of what He's doing on the earth, in His people.

> You can't be a peacemaker if you don't know the Prince of Peace who abides in you.

Let me add that being a peacemaker is more than keeping people from fighting. That's keeping the peace. Jesus didn't say blessed are the peacekeepers; He said blessed are the peacemakers. Peacekeepers maintain the peace already there; peacemakers bring peace into any situation. Jesus was the ultimate peacemaker. He was an offering for peace when He died on the cross. Romans 16:20 says, "The God of peace will soon crush Satan under your feet."

God, from the beginning, had one purpose: to make man in His image. We see, throughout the ages, God has been working with His people, speaking to them, directing them, always with this one thought in mind. He sent His Son, Jesus, and the first thing

He did was establish the attitudes of what a Son of God will be.

Isaiah 53 is a picture of the heart of Jesus.

When Jesus came, He came to clarify the attitudes we are to have. He came to satisfy the reason God made man. Jesus began with the disciples, defining the heart attitudes of sons and daughters of God. Isaiah 53 is a picture of the heart of Jesus. In Isaiah 53, we see Jesus from the inside out. It is one of the most profound pictures of Christ's life in the whole of the Scriptures.

When I was first pastoring, I recorded myself reading seven or eight translations (the New American Standard, New English Bible, Amplified Bible, and so on) of Isaiah 53. Everywhere I went for about a month, I played that recording of Isaiah 53 because it showed me the heart of Christ. (These days, apps that enable you to listen to Scripture on your phone make this much easier.)

Do you want to know the heart of Christ? Do you want to know the way to His power and authority? Do you want to know true spiritual maturity? Isaiah 53 says:

> Who has believed our report? And to whom has the arm of the Lord been revealed? For He grew

up before Him like a tender shoot, and like a root out of dry ground; He has no stately form or majesty that we would look at Him, nor an appearance that we would take pleasure in Him. He was despised and abandoned by men, a man of great pain and familiar with sickness; and like one from whom people hide their faces, He was despised, and we had no regard for Him.

However, it was our sicknesses that He Himself bore, and our pains that He carried; yet we ourselves assumed that He had been afflicted, struck down by God, and humiliated. But He was pierced for our offenses, He was crushed for our wrongdoings; the punishment for our well-being was laid upon Him, and by His wounds we are healed. All of us, like sheep, have gone astray, each of us has turned to his own way; but the Lord has caused the wrong-doing of us all to fall on Him.

He was oppressed and afflicted, yet He did not open His mouth; like a lamb that is led to slaughter, and like a sheep that is silent before its shearers, so He did not open His mouth. By oppression and judgment He was taken away; and as for His generation, who considered that He was cut off from the land of the living for the wrongdoing of my people, to whom the blow was due? And His grave was assigned with wicked men, yet He was with a rich man in His death, because He had done no violence, nor was there any deceit in His mouth.

But the Lord desired to crush Him, causing Him grief; if He renders Himself as a guilt offering, He will see His offspring, He will prolong His days, and the good pleasure of the Lord will prosper in His hand. As a result of the anguish of His soul, He will see it and be satisfied; by His knowledge the Righteous One, My Servant, will justify the many, for He will bear their wrongdoings. Therefore, I will allot Him a portion with the great, and He will divide the plunder with the strong, because He poured out His life unto death, and was counted with wrongdoers; yet He Himself bore the sin of many, and interceded for the wrongdoers.

—ISAIAH 53:1–12

Isaiah 53 is a prophecy about Jesus' suffering. He came as a man, tempted in all things, such as we are, and yet without sin. The Word says, "He was despised and rejected by mankind" (Isa. 53:3, NIV). It speaks about how He bore our sorrows, "yet we considered him punished by God, stricken by Him, and afflicted" (v. 4, NIV).

He came into the same world we live in—with conflict and injustice. But He showed us in Isaiah 53 how to deal with the conditions of the world around Him. It speaks of what happened to Him. He was cut off from the land of the living, He was quiet before His shearers as a lamb led to the slaughter, and He was taken away. It says in verse 10 (NIV),

Yet it was the LORD's will to crush him and cause
him to suffer, and though the LORD makes his
life an offering for sin, he will see his offspring
and prolong his days, and the will of the LORD
will prosper in his hand.

Jesus is the pattern son. He offered Himself to
God as a sacrifice. When people criticized Him and
said, "You're smitten of God," He did not reply. While
being reviled, He did not revile in return. When being
threatened, He uttered no threats. He kept entrusting
Himself to Him who judges righteously. He continued
to offer Himself to God for the wrong things around
Him. He rendered Himself a guilt offering.

When you see wrong things, when you have been
wronged, the response of a mature Christian, a son or
daughter of God, is to render yourself to God. "Lord,
how can I make this thing right? How can I be that
reflection of Jesus Christ into this world?" You say,
"Francis, are you talking about us atoning for people's
sins? Are you talking about us taking Jesus' place?" No.
I'm talking about Jesus taking our place. I'm talking
about Jesus' life, Jesus' love, and Jesus' character
coming forth through us in such a tangible way that it
releases the hand of God.

He said that if He would render Himself as a guilt
offering for all those wrong things, then the power of
God "will prosper in His hand." That's what I want. I
want Christ's redemptive power to prosper.

"But Francis, Isaiah 53 is talking about Jesus." No. It's not only talking about Jesus. He said that if He rendered Himself as a guilt offering, He would see His offspring. *You, the church, are His offspring:* people who think, love, and act like Him. Jesus went to the cross as a single man. He did not have physical children. You are the offspring of Christ's sacrifice. The life of Jesus coming forth through you produces maturity and sonship so that when you look at the condition of the world, you're not just judging it.

From the time I first got saved, people have told me what is wrong with the world. I've seen God—not in physical form, but I've seen His heart. When God sees our cities, I know He wants to bring mercy. He wants people willing to pay the price to see their world change the way His Son paid the price to see His world change.

Philippians chapter 2 says, "Have this attitude in yourselves which was also in Christ Jesus, who, as He already existed in the form of God, did not consider equality with God something to be grasped, but emptied Himself" of His position, of His privileges, and He poured Himself out and became "obedient to the point of death: death on a cross" (vv. 5–8).

In every generation, God has His people who have been cleansed, repented of sin, and given themselves to the process of becoming pure. His people pay the price and lay down their lives for the world around them the way He laid down His life for us.

The first one to give their life for Jesus was Stephen, and Stephen was following the pattern of His Master. He was a son. While they stoned him to death, Stephen looked up. He saw Jesus standing and said, "Lord, do not hold this sin against them!" (Acts 7:60). He absorbed that sin. He turned the other cheek. He prayed for those who were persecuting him. He surrendered the right to judge, the right to be angry, and the right to fight back. He surrendered the right to defend himself because he rejected that need of human escape.

Instead, he chose to escape by way of love. He said, "Lord, do not hold this sin against them." The hand of God, the arm of the Lord, reached down and touched a man standing there. Paul would later become the greatest apostle there ever was, and he witnessed the stoning of Stephen.

> *Lord, help me to escape by way of love. Teach me to surrender my right to judge, be angry, and fight back. Please help me to be a peacemaker instead.*

CHAPTER 16

THE PERSECUTED

*Blessed are those who are persecuted because of
righteousness, for theirs is the kingdom of heaven.*
—MATTHEW 5:10, NIV

s I BEGIN this chapter on persecution, I want to clarify what it is *not* talking about. If we view the Beatitudes as a progression, it becomes obvious that verse 10 does not apply to someone who has not yet gone through the sequence of discovering your need, repenting, and becoming humble.

Oftentimes, some of the problems we call persecution might be self-inflicted. We can suffer from a general lack of grace, love, wisdom, and even a lack of Jesus. It turns people off when we come in His name without His nature. So, we can get criticized for the lack of Jesus as much as for the fullness of Jesus. And I want to separate those categories.

I also want to clarify that there's never been a command in the Bible where God said to any of His saints, "I want you to persecute somebody else." You might know Christians who feel anointed to persecute, but the Scripture says in Galatians that "he who was born after the flesh persecuted him who was born after the Spirit" (Gal. 4:29, MEV).

So, you'll find that those born of the Spirit never get into the realm of persecution. They might speak the truth in love and confront wrong things, but they won't get into a crusade against someone or something.

Last, we must be honest about the struggle in this sequence that God is working within us. We must recognize that the word *struggle* is part of the Christian experience. It goes back to the difference between conversion and discipleship. Salvation is free because

Jesus paid for it, but the kingdom of God costs you everything—and it does not come with a money-back guarantee. You've got to give your all and keep giving it until you get what God has for you.

Salvation is free because Jesus paid for it, but the kingdom of God costs you everything—and it does not come with a money-back guarantee.

That's why there's a struggle involved in the stages. And in that struggle, things break down in us—things like our pride and that separation that the human soul has from tragedy until we are touched by the pain of life. When that shell of superficiality—that little fragile thing that keeps us from truly feeling other people's needs—is broken down, we gain a new understanding and connection with those in pain. For example, once somebody close to you has cancer, suddenly *cancer* is a terrifying word. It's not a word you joke about because it's personal and carries an intimacy that is painful. It's the same thing when it comes to sin.

When becoming Christlike, you embrace the struggle of walking through life without fear. You embrace the struggle of walking without lust and all the sins common to humanity. You get into the pain, the stumbling and rising, the fight. You get into the depth of repentance, and suddenly, when you look at somebody going through that, you're not standing back judging them.

The Christian pharisee judges harshly because he's never had a personal experience with the struggle of getting the roots of sin out and truly repenting. He doesn't have compassion for the struggle. He can't relate to a disciple's freedom when they truly repent and God removes the stain of sin from their heart. He doesn't have humility. He stands dressed in self-righteousness, pointing the finger without ever having a real, intimate knowledge of all that it means to come into purity of heart.

The persecution referenced in the Beatitudes is not about the self-righteous people who have not passed through the cross or felt the pain of struggle. Unless we go through those things, we're not enough of a threat for the enemy to hunt and begin a slander campaign against us. The persecution Jesus spoke of is the culmination of going through all God has brought us through, leading us to see God.

Right now, the enemy doesn't fear the church because the church doesn't fear the Lord. But when the church fears God, the enemy fears the church. The church that sees God is a tremendous threat to the devil because the power of God is now able to be released.

If you've progressed this far in the sequence of transformation, you're becoming a threat to the enemy. You're becoming a son of God, a peace offering. Jesus is a peacemaker, but He's also a peace offering. You are developing spiritual authority. You see God, so you have the desire to make peace where there is conflict. You are extending the kingdom of God wherever you walk; you're the frontier of the kingdom of God. That is something Satan persecutes.

THE ENEMY'S TACTICS FOR PERSECUTION

The way Satan persecutes is described in Matthew 5:11 (MEV): "Blessed are you when men revile you, and persecute you, and say all kinds of evil against you falsely for My sake."

We need to tune in to several things here. First, the Scripture says, "All who desire to live a godly life in Christ Jesus will suffer persecution" (2 Tim. 3:12, MEV). So, it's not a matter of *if* you will be persecuted, but *when.* Maybe it will come from a family member or friend, a coworker or teammate. Wherever it comes from, it is legitimate persecution. You're trying to live holy and righteous before the Lord, and then you are persecuted for it.

Understand that the enemy has designed persecution to immobilize you. If the enemy cannot take your life, he will try to crush parts of your life that render you ineffective. He wants to steal your joy because the joy of the Lord is your strength. When criticism or other forms of persecution come, Jesus is saying,

"Rejoice and be glad." He knows the enemy's tactics, but He does not want them to stop you in your walk with God.

When the enemy persecuted me, I would park there and get depressed. Finally, the Lord spoke to my heart during a time when I was really stressed, and He said, "Rejoice and leap for joy." I knew at the time the Lord wanted me to dance to break the oppression. That spirit of heaviness would not lift until I danced before the Lord, so I did. I just leaped about. Thank goodness the drapes were closed because I probably looked crazy. But I began to leap for joy because the Lord showed me that the enemy brought on that persecution to steal my joy.

Luke says to leap for joy. That word means to bound about with joy. At times, that much joy is necessary to cast off heaviness. It's heaviness designed by the enemy to stop you in your walk with God, and the joy of the Lord is the antidote.

If you've been feeling the heaviness of persecution, leap for joy. Please don't allow it to stop you in your journey to Christlikeness. You've done much work to get to where the enemy hates you. Don't blow it now by getting depressed about it! If he persecutes you, take it as a sign that you're doing something right. Don't slow down. Begin to rejoice. Begin to leap for joy.

The next thing the enemy will try to do is cloud your credibility with suspicion and innuendo. If his first tactic didn't work, the next assault comes to silence you through faultfinding and accusation.

For example, he may have someone criticize you or talk about you behind your back. And it doesn't even have to be a lie about you. It's bad enough when people lie about you. What's worse is when they tell the truth about you! They talk about things you really did, some of which you may have repented for.

God forgets it. But who remembers it? The accuser of the brethren. He takes some of the things you did wrong, even after you've repented and received forgiveness, and uses them against you.

Revelation 12 provides an insightful picture of the accuser of the brethren coming after you as God's servant. It talks about a man-child and a dragon seeking to devour him, but verse 5 says the child "was caught up to God and to His throne." It's widely accepted that this refers to Jesus Christ.

I agree that it refers to Jesus, but I think there are applications to be made here that when you're under accusation, the only safe place from the mouth of the accuser, the mouth of the dragon who wants to swallow you up, is to get caught up to God in His throne. God's presence is the only place of peace, refuge, security, and contentment. Think of persecution as the jet fuel to get you there.

"Great is your reward" (Matt. 5:12, NIV). The reward He refers to is in verse 10, "[Yours] is the kingdom of heaven." He's saying, "The enemy's coming to distract you. He's coming to drag you off and take over your thoughts, to expend your energy. The only safe place is God's throne."

If you've done something wrong, repent of it. But when the accuser comes and you've examined your personal life and done all you can to deal with those accusations, you've got to get to God's throne and lay it at His feet. That's your place of safety.

THE PATH TO HIS PRESENCE

"But Francis," one might ask, "how do I get to His throne?" Worship is the pathway to His presence. You begin to worship, praise Him for who He is. Thank Him for His goodness and mercy and all His mighty works, then approach Him on behalf of those who persecute you, because part of being at God's throne is being there with Christ, who is ever living to make intercession for the saints. The nature of Christ is to pray for those who persecute. So, the way out of persecution is to get to the throne where God's presence surrounds you.

God never intended for us to do His will without His presence. The power to accomplish God's purpose comes from prayer and intimacy with Him. It is here, closed in with God, where we find an ever-replenishing flow of spiritual virtue.

In my book *The Three Battlegrounds*, I put it this way:

Without true worship of God there can be no victory in warfare. For what we bleed when we are wounded by satanic assault or persecution is the true measure of our worship. You see, what comes out of our hearts during times of pressure is in us, but it's hidden during times of ease. If you are a true worshipper, your spirit will exude worship to God no matter what battle you are fighting. In warfare, worship creates a wall of fire around the soul.

I surrender, Lord! I give myself to You and enlist in Your army of worshippers. I choose to praise You and increase Your shelter around me with the worship I give to You. You are my purpose for living.

CHAPTER 17

GREAT IS YOUR REWARD

Rejoice and be glad, because great is your reward in heaven, for in the same way they perse- cuted the prophets who were before you.

—MATTHEW 5:12, NIV

I N THE PREVIOUS chapter we looked at the various forms of persecution the enemy will throw at us. We also found the antidote to persecution in Jesus' command to "rejoice and be glad" (Matt. 5:12). If we read the rest of verse 12, we discover that we will receive the same great reward as those who were persecuted before us.

There is a sequence for those God uses to speak to nations, those God anoints to get to the place where they truly represent Him. There are those who operate with the gift of prophecy and those who hold the prophetic office.

The Beatitudes reveal to us the characteristics of a New Testament prophet. The New Testament prophet is not a Jeremiah type, anointed to pluck up, tear down, and destroy.

The Old Testament had prophets like Samuel, the leader of what was called the school of the prophets. When Jesus came, He taught the Sermon on the Mount; He set up the standards of the New Testament prophetic ministry and what the New Testament prophet will look like.

If you have come to the point where your heart is so fine-tuned by humility that you tremble at the whisper of God, then you have learned to recognize the Lord's voice. Showing faithfulness in the little things required, you continue to progress through the Beatitudes, your eye is open, and you see God. Somebody who sees

God, the Bible calls a seer. Somebody who hears God is, generally speaking, a prophet.

He says, "They persecuted the prophets who were before you."

I believe the Beatitudes are a sequence to building the character of a New Testament prophet. Maybe you don't fully agree with this interpretation, but I want to say regardless of what a person's ministry is—evangelist, pastor, apostle, teacher—everyone must go through that process to get there. We all do if we are to be disciples made in the image of Jesus Christ.

The height of what gives pleasure to God is the worshipping hearts of His servants who willingly lay down their lives. With hearts that ascend amid persecution, they come before God and love Him with a precious kind of devotion—it's this heart that angels long to gaze into. It's why God created man.

When you look at Jesus—our model, our pattern, the virtue bearer, the vine that supplies us life—you find that at the height of being persecuted, having been maligned and lied about, He went to the cross. If you read Psalm 22, it looks right into everything Jesus is saying on the cross. It starts, "My God, my God, why have You forsaken Me?" (v. 1, NKJV). It goes on, "They pierced My hands and My feet. I can count all My bones....They divide My garments among them" (vv. 16–18, NKJV). It's a picture of Christ.

But then, right there in the middle, as He's crying out, He says, "I will praise Thee." He begins to praise, and you hear, "From the horns of the wild oxen! You have answered Me" (v. 21, NKJV). On the verge of death, Jesus reconnects in worship to the Father. First and foremost, the Son of God on the cross having been misjudged, having laid His life down as the peace offering for the world's sins—that worship on the cross amid being reviled gave the Father the highest pleasure God could draw from His creation.

We also, in following Christ's example, worship God in the midst of trials and sufferings; even if unjustly or innocently, with hearts bowed and surrendered we can bring pleasure to the heart of the Father.

Jesus tells us to take up our cross if we are to follow Him. What does the cross, this persecution represent? It represents lives that have determined that God alone is the reason we live. It represents lives that say, "I will not live for the glory of man." It represents individuals who have been delivered from the illusion that "self" is worth keeping. As individuals, we see who God is and why we live.

When you're the object of someone's criticism, seize the opportunity, and offer to God worship—for yours is the kingdom of heaven. What you're giving to God is why He made men: to offer praise in spite of your circumstances!

When the Lord brought Israel out of Egypt, He said He wanted them to worship Him in the wilderness, and then they would go in and take the Promised

Land. He promised them they would enter "a land flowing with milk and honey" (Deut. 27:3, NKJV).

He takes us into battle and conflict until we worship Him in the midst of it. Our promised land is the presence of God. We can't find our land of milk and honey, the presence of God, until we worship Him amid the wilderness of conflict and strife.

The Lord is concerned about fulfilling our desires, but to do so, He must pry our fingers off our lives and turn our hearts toward Him. Indeed, the reason we are alive is not to fulfill our desires but to become His worshippers.

Personal fulfillment can become an idol; it can develop into such an obsession that we live for happiness more than God. Thus, part of our salvation includes having our desires prioritized by Christ. Later in the Sermon on the Mount, Jesus put it this way: "Seek first His kingdom and His righteousness, and all these things will be provided to you. So do not worry about tomorrow; for tomorrow will worry about itself" (Matt. 6:33–34). God will satisfy our desires and needs, but not before He is first in our hearts.

GENUINE WORSHIP CAUSES US TO BECOME GENUINE CHRISTIANS

We have heard that God desires to have a relationship with us, and this is true. But it is our nature that defines this relationship as one that is perfectly accommodating, casual, and mostly defined by our terms and needs. Yes, God desires that our union with Him be full and wonderful. Yet His descent into our lives, His commitment to redeem and restore us, has another purpose: the reality of His presence transforms us into worshippers.

Indeed, worship is the evidence of a transformed, Christlike life. Worship might be expressed with tears of joy or in silent awe; it might create an abiding gratitude toward God or inspire songs in the night. Regardless of the form of expression, the worship the Father seeks is meaningful. It turns our complete being toward God in love.

> Worship is the evidence of a
> transformed, Christlike life.

If, however, the idea of worship seems strange, if it feels mechanical or if the words expressed seem hollow, that means we need to go deeper into God's Word to get to know Him. The closer we draw to God, the more we are transformed; the greater our transformation, the more completely we respond in worship. True worship deepens and matures as we walk with God.

Worship is a choice we make. I choose to worship to demonstrate my trust in God when my circumstances appear hostile; I choose to worship by burrowing into the heart of God when all around me is in turmoil. And as I'm lifted into His presence, I am also aware that the character of my life is being measured by my worship at His altar.

Lord, come into my life and fulfill Your promise of transformation. Create praise on my lips and help me worship You in spirit and truth.

CHAPTER 18

THE MIRACLE ZONE

Jesus was going about in all of Galilee, teaching in their synagogues and proclaiming the gospel of the kingdom and healing every disease and every sickness among the people.

—MATTHEW 4:23

THROUGHOUT THIS BOOK we've looked at three basic categories of Christians. The largest group consists of people who try to avoid the darkness in the world but have no hope that the world can be redeemed. Assuming Christ's return is imminent, they retreat into what seems a shelter of apathy concerning the non-Christian world around them. They have not surrendered themselves to the course of transformation. Their souls are vexed by the conduct of unprincipled men (2 Pet. 2:7–8). Their compassion is kindled but limited. Rarely do they extend themselves beyond the needs of their immediate family and closest friends. They love the Lord, but they don't know how to change society or what to do to positively impact their world.

The second group of Christians consists of those who would rather rail at the darkness than adjust to it. Though much smaller in number than the first, they are by no means apathetic; in fact, they appear the opposite. They rage at the depravity of the ungodly and protest the audacity of the wicked. They pound the pulpit and pavement, both vocal and visible. Yet their ability to transform their culture is, for the most part, neutralized by their negativity and rage. They are dismissed as judgmental extremists. Most sinners cannot endure the harshness of their approach.

Both groups sincerely desire to see our culture transformed. Yet the same problem afflicts them: they are troubled that the world is unchristian without being troubled that their hearts are un-Christlike. They do not perceive the priority of God's heart, which is the transformation of the church into the image of Christ (Rom. 8:28–29).

WORLD CHANGERS NEEDED

This passion to be conformed to Christ separates the third group from the others. Though the smallest in number, its members are the most effective. Throughout history, these have been the world changers. These are the individuals who have understood the priority of God. They know that the Father's highest passion is to behold His Son revealed in a believer's soul. As much as they are moved with compassion for the lost, their primary quest is not only to touch their neighbors' hearts but to touch the heart of God. They know that if they awaken the Father's pleasure, the power of His Spirit will go before them. God Himself will change the hearts of those around them.

It is my sincere quest in life to be like Jesus in everything. It stuns me to know that if I am truly conformed to Christ, I have the Spirit's promise that I will also awaken the pleasure of almighty God. As we embrace transformation, the power to touch cities and redeem cultures is also there, for it takes transformed people to transform nations.

TO BE LIKE CHRIST

Indeed, this hunger for Christlikeness was the secret of Paul's success. His expressed vision was simply "that I may know Him and the power of His resurrection and the fellowship of His sufferings, being conformed to His death" (Phil. 3:10).

Paul's passion was taken up with this one heavenly goal: "being conformed" to the life and power of Jesus Christ. The apostle's quest was not only to win the world but also to know Jesus Christ. The works Paul accomplished—founding churches, writing almost half the New Testament, winning the lost, demonstrating miraculous spiritual gifts, and remaining faithful throughout times of terrible suffering—were all by-products of his passion for knowing Christ.

Likewise, with us, the Father's immediate, primary goal for the church is for us to be like His Son. He rescues us so He can transform us. Some say that the Father's goal is to win the lost. Yet if this were His highest priority, He would simply bypass the church and save men Himself.

Has He not proved, as seen in Paul's conversion, that His abilities to save people are without limit? Did He not change the arrogant heart of King Nebuchadnezzar into a man of meekness who gave glory to God? Who can resist Him who is irresistible? However, instead of revealing His glory, He chooses to reach the lost through the agency of transformed people.

This, my friend, is the glorious mystery of our existence: the Almighty has purposed from eternity to create a race of men and women who, though tested in a corrupt and violent world, bear the image and likeness of Christ (Gen. 1:27). Christ calls this heavenly natured people, the church, His "new creation" (2 Cor. 5:17).

This, my friend, is the glorious mystery of our existence: the Almighty has purposed from eternity to create a race of men and women who, though tested in a corrupt and violent world, bear the image and likeness of Christ (Gen. 1:27).

The life of Christ, unveiled against the backdrop of humanity's need, is the most compelling reality in the universe. Indeed, when Jesus is lifted up, people from all cultures are universally drawn to Him (John 12:32).

Such was the case at the commencement of His ministry. We read that "news about Him spread throughout Syria" and "large crowds followed Him from Galilee and the Decapolis, and Jerusalem, and Judea, and from beyond the Jordan" (Matt. 4:24–25). Multitudes, not only from Israel but also from the surrounding gentile world, thronged to see the Son of God.

Imagine attending a crusade where Jesus Himself healed the masses and delivered people of "every disease and every sickness" (Matt. 4:23)! Lepers with missing body parts, clothed in rags, shuffling up to the healing lines. At the touch of Jesus, instantly healing flowed into their bodies! The blind, deaf, and dumb left their encounter with Jesus seeing, hearing, and shouting their praise to God; demoniacs and those tormented by mental anguish found peace and deliverance.

Who wouldn't come to see such a move of God?

Wherever Jesus stood, heaven manifested on earth in that time and place. It was as though the eternal kingdom of God focused a powerful spotlight on Israel's Messiah. Anywhere within this cone of light that surrounded Jesus became a miracle zone. It did not matter what condition or illness compelled people toward Christ. Even those who crept forward secretly from behind Him—all found healing! Demons fled howling as the oppressed entered the spotlight of God.

The terminal post for that healing power, of course, was Jesus. The holy current of God's Spirit poured through the uniquely prepared heart of the Son of God. Indeed, the closer they came to the Messiah, the stronger their anticipation became that all things were possible with God.

Today, despite the advance of militant darkness, humanity's Savior remains focused on reaching the lost. Yes, even while iniquity abounds and the love of many grows cold, and despite false prophets leading many astray, the God of heaven is establishing the initial stages of His kingdom (Dan. 2:44). And many hungry Christians are seeking first the kingdom of God and His righteousness. Indeed, Jesus said that prior to the rapture, heaven's gospel would be proclaimed in every nation "and then the end will come" (Matt. 24:14).

THE KINGDOM WITHIN YOU

Finally, do not fret if others fail to see what you see concerning the kingdom of God. When the Pharisees questioned Jesus "as to when the kingdom of God was coming," Jesus answered, "The kingdom of God is not coming with signs that can be observed; nor will they say, 'Look, here it is!' or, 'There it is!' For behold, the kingdom of God is [within you]" (Luke 17:20–21).

The Pharisees asked Him *when* the kingdom of God was coming; Jesus told them *where*. It will first come within the hearts of His followers. Yes, it will ultimately fill the earth with the glory of God. Yet, in its initial manifestation, it comes to create attitudes that prepare men and women for the physical return of Christ.

Today, a powerful shift is occurring. The focus of many Christians' hearts has moved from a traditional, once-a-week church service to daily seeking God's kingdom restored. As we progress into the reality of the kingdom, we will see the "miracle zone" return.

"For the kingdom of God is not in words, but in power" (1 Cor. 4:20). And the first place the power of God seeks to accomplish its marvelous work is in conforming our hearts to the attitudes of the kingdom.

> *Lord, I look forward to the day when Your glory will fill the whole earth. Until then, let me be part of the shift You are creating. Let me be part of the miracle zone that brings Your power and Your kingdom reality into every situation.*

CONCLUSION

SWALLOWED UP IN LIFE

TWO FORCES ARE increasing in the world: the power of life and the power of death. The Scriptures tell us that before Christ returns, Satan will be cast down from the spirit realm to the earthly realm "with great wrath, knowing that he has only a short time" (Rev. 12:12). Jesus warns us in Matthew 24:22 that "if those days had not been cut short, no life would have been saved." Prophecy after prophecy warns of these days. Satanic darkness is on the face of the earth, and where the devil is, death and destruction are soon to follow.

At the same time, the sons of the kingdom should expect to enter ever-increasing degrees of life. Through repentance and faith in God's Word, we are seeing more of the Holy Spirit and more of Christ's presence restored to the church. I believe before Jesus returns, the church will be measurably as full of life as Christ was when He walked in His earthly ministry.

Paul tells us that a time will come when "what is mortal is swallowed up by life" (2 Cor. 5:4). As the last trumpet sounds, our perishable bodies will "put on the imperishable, and this mortal must put on immortality" (1 Cor. 15:53). Think about it: immortality, death, and decay swallowed up by life! We are not facing death; we are discarding death. We are facing *life*—abundant, eternal, and indestructible!

This is important for us to grasp because what seems to occur "in a moment, in the twinkling of an eye" (1 Cor. 15:52) is actually the result of years of progressively laying down our self-lives and progressively absorbing and living in Christ's life. The Scripture tells us, "For you have died, and your life is hidden with Christ in God. When Christ, *who is our life,* is revealed, then you also will be revealed with Him in glory" (Col. 3:3–4, emphasis added). The key to the revealed glory is the hidden life we share daily with Christ. It must be a true statement: Christ is my life—in my home, my hopes, my heart, my future, and all my relationships. At the same time, we must honestly face the fact that there are areas in us in which Christ is not yet our life. And we must do something about it.

We are not facing death; we
are discarding death.

THE HIDDEN MANNA

Although life is obviously within and around us, Jesus said, "Few are they who find it." Most people just exist. They go through their days afraid to live and afraid to die. We need to know that the life Christ came to give us doesn't automatically fall on us like the sunshine and rain He gives; God hides His life in His will. And if we would find His life, we must do His will.

In Revelation 2:17, Jesus promised, "To the one who overcomes, I will give some of the hidden manna." The life God has for us is hidden. Jesus called the kingdom of God "a treasure hidden in the field" (Matt. 13:44). Even though life is within and around us, we must search for it like fine gold and dig for it like silver.

Additionally, Solomon tells us that "God made men upright, but they have sought out many schemes" (Eccles. 7:29). There is something contrary about human nature that, even though we love light, we are bent toward darkness. We want relationships with people but don't want to maintain them. It is so easy for a man to come home and look at his wife as one of the "things" in the home. "There's the chair, the couch, the table, my wife, the lamp." A man must cultivate being sensitive to the person of his wife.

On the other hand, women complain that their husbands don't communicate with them. When he finally does talk, she ruins it by telling him how often he fails to meet her needs. It is so easy to blame others for our failure to relate, but the problem is latent within us all. We desire love but often fail to give it! It would be safe to say all of us need God's help.

In the Book of Daniel, the angel Gabriel approached the prophet to give him understanding concerning a vision. Daniel explained his reaction to this supernatural encounter. He said, "Now while he was talking with me, I was dazed with my face to the ground" (Dan. 8:18). Every time God deals with your heart and touches you, He is making you stand upright. When I see you cry during worship, I know that the very Spirit of God

Himself is waking you and pulling your face up off the earth. And when your heart is burning within you at the reading or preaching of the Word, it is nothing less than Christ Himself making you stand upright.

Don't be afraid of letting the Lord touch you. Don't let defeats, failings, or circumstances keep you from remaining open to the Lord. More life is coming! More of His presence is at hand! Stay vulnerable to Him, and He will progressively pour more of heaven's power into your life. And as you continue to seek Him for His life in your relationships, gradually you will see your human attitudes becoming more divine. In a moment, in the twinkling of an eye, you will see that which is mortal being swallowed up by life!

NOTES

CHAPTER 4

1. "Mark 2:1–3:6—Jesus Clashes With Religious 'Experts,'" Christian Study Library, accessed November 15, 2023, https://www.christianstudylibrary.org/article/mark-21–36-jesus-clashes-religious-"experts".

CHAPTER 12

1. "Bible Commentaries: Genesis 1," StudyLight.org, accessed November 15, 2023, http://www.studylight.org/com/acc/view.cgi?book=ge&chapter=001.

1.

ABOUT THE AUTHOR

FRANCIS FRANGIPANE RECEIVED ministerial training at Grace Chapel in Southern California. He and his wife, Denise, started their first church in Hilo, Hawaii. From there they pastored a small church in Detroit and planted eight churches and home groups in southeastern Michigan and Ontario, Canada.

Later, Frangipane accepted a position pastoring a church in Cedar Rapids, Iowa. It was in Iowa that Frangipane became united with several other pastors from various evangelical denominations who met for monthly prayer. After three years, the founding minister of this prayer group moved, and Frangipane and another local pastor picked up the prayer initiative. They opened it up for intercessors and increased their times together from monthly to weekly. The group multiplied, which led to many other interdenominational citywide events.

It was also during this time that Frangipane began to write. His first book, *Holiness, Truth and the Presence of God*, was a compilation of his essays and sermons. That and his second book, *The Three Battlegrounds*, became best sellers. He has written fifteen books, including four training manuals developed for his online school In Christ's Image Training, plus a number of study booklets.

Frangipane is the founder of River of Life Ministries and has traveled throughout the world ministering to thousands of pastors and intercessors from many backgrounds. His heartfelt prayer is to see Christlike pastors and intercessors united before God, revealing the love of Christ to their communities.

Over the past decades, Frangipane has served on a number of ministry boards and is the president of In Christ's Image Training, an online discipleship program. He is currently devoting himself to prayer and the ministry of God's Word, and his daughter, Joy, works alongside him as he continues to seek the heart of God.